CONTEMPORARY GERMAN WRITERS

HANS-ULRICH TREICHEL

Series Editor

Rhys W. Williams has been Professor of German and Head of the German Department at University of Wales Swansea since 1984. He has published extensively on the literature of German Expressionism and on the post-war novel. He is Director of the Centre for Contemporary German Literature at University of Wales Swansea.

CONTEMPORARY GERMAN WRITERS

Series Editor: Rhys W. Williams

HANS-ULRICH TREICHEL

edited by

David Basker

CARDIFF
UNIVERSITY OF WALES PRESS
2004

© The Contributors, 2004

British Library Cataloguing-in-Publication Data
A catalogue record for this book is available from the British Library.

ISBN   0-7083-1716-2 paperback
       0-7083-1715-4 hardback

All rights reserved. No part of this book may be reproduced, stored in a retrieval system, or transmitted, in any form or by any means, electronic, mechanical, photocopying, recording or otherwise, without clearance from the University of Wales Press, 10 Columbus Walk, Brigantine Place, Cardiff, CF10 4UP.
www.wales.ac.uk/press

The right of the Contributors to be identified separately as authors of this work has been asserted by them in accordance with sections 77 and 79 of the Copyright, Designs and Patents Act 1988.

Printed in Great Britain by Dinefwr Press, Llandybïe.

Contents

	page
List of Contributors	vii
Preface	ix
Abbreviations	xi

1 Gedichte
   Hans-Ulrich Treichel   1

2 Hans-Ulrich Treichel: Outline Biography
   David Basker   10

3 »Leseerfahrungen sind Lebenserfahrungen«: Gespräch mit Hans-Ulrich Treichel
   Rhys W. Williams   12

4 »Wenn du bedürftig bist, sinken deine Chancen«: Der Erzähler Hans-Ulrich Treichel zwischen Wirklichkeit und Vorstellung
   Stephan Reinhardt   28

5 'Schlüsselszenen der Erfahrung': (Dis)location in the Prose Work of Hans-Ulrich Treichel
   David Basker   37

6 Guilt and Shame in Hans-Ulrich Treichel's *Der Verlorene*
   David Clarke   61

7 'sehnsüchtig-traurig und unerlöst': Memory's Longing to Forget. Or Why *Tristanakkord* is not Simply a Reprise of Martin Walser
   Stuart Taberner   79

8 'Caravaggio in Preußen': Hans-Ulrich Treichel's *Der irdische Amor*
   Rhys W. Williams   94

9 Bibliography
    David Basker   111

Index   137

List of Contributors

David Basker is Senior Lecturer in German at University of Wales Swansea. His study *Chaos, Control and Consistency: The Narrative Vision of Wolfgang Koeppen* appeared in 1993. He has published on all aspects of Koeppen's literary career and has edited the *Sarah Kirsch, Uwe Timm* and *Hermann Peter Piwitt* volumes in the Contemporary German Writers series.

David Clarke is Lecturer in German at the University of Bath. He studied at the Universities of Leeds, London (UCL) and Wales (Swansea). His main research interests are the literature of the GDR, German film and contemporary German literature. He is author of the monograph *'Diese merkwürdige Kleinigkeit einer Vision': Christoph Hein's Social Critique in Transition* (2002) and articles on the writers Christian Kracht and Reinhard Jirgl.

Stephan Reinhardt lives in Heidelberg and is a broadcaster, editor and literary critic. He reviews extensively for the press and radio in German-speaking countries. Among his recent publications is his acclaimed biography of Alfred Andersch.

Stuart Taberner is Senior Lecturer in German at the University of Leeds. Educated at the Universities of Cambridge and Chicago, he also worked as lecturer in German at the University of Bristol. His research focuses on the relationships between politics and writing, the role of the German intellectual in the period after 1945, and literature published since 1989. He has published on the Holocaust, its impact on post-unification Germany, 'normalization' and national identity, and relationships between Germans and Jews, as expressed in film, literature and intellectual debate.

Rhys W. Williams is Professor of German at the University of Wales Swansea and Director of the Centre for Contemporary German Literature. He has published extensively on German Expressionism (Sternheim, Benn, Carl Einstein and Toller) and on contemporary literature (Andersch, Böll, Schneider, Timm, Treichel, Martin Walser).

Preface

Contemporary German Writers

Each volume of the Contemporary German Writers series is devoted to an author who has spent a period as Visiting Writer at the Centre for Contemporary German Literature in the Department of German at the University of Wales Swansea. The first chapter in each volume contains an original, previously unpublished piece by the writer concerned; the second consists of a biographical sketch, outlining the main events of the author's life and setting the works in context, particularly for the non-specialist or general reader. A third chapter will, in each case, contain an interview with the author, normally conducted during the writer's stay in Swansea. Subsequent chapters will contain contributions by invited British and German academics and critics on aspects of the writer's œuvre. While each volume will seek to provide both an overview of the author and some detailed analysis of individual works, the nature of that critical engagement will inevitably depend on the relative importance of the author concerned and on the amount of critical material which his or her work has previously inspired. Each volume includes an extensive bibliography designed to fill any gaps or remedy deficiencies in existing bibliographies. The intention is to produce in each case a book which will serve both as an introduction to the writer concerned and as a resource for specialists in contemporary German literature.

Hans-Ulrich Treichel

The current volume begins with nine previously unpublished poems by Hans-Ulrich Treichel, which include reflections on the author's childhood, on his personal development and on his family history. There follows a biographical sketch and an interview with Treichel which, as well as addressing each of his major publications, sheds light on the origins of his literary career and on the relationship between creative writing and academic work. The interview is followed by a survey of the whole of Treichel's career by the noted literary critic Stephan Reinhardt, who values in particular the author's theory-free 'Sinn für Affekte und Effekte'. David Basker then focuses on the presentation of geographical setting in Treichel's prose works, identifying the sense of being out of place in one's environment as a fundamental creative impulse. There follow three chapters focusing on specific works. David Clarke examines the presentation of guilt and shame in *Der Verlorene* and argues that, while these emotional conditions are common to all three protagonists, the experiences which trigger them are different. Treichel's book thus calls into question the roles of these emotions in creating a unified national response to the trauma of the past. Stuart Taberner takes as the starting point for his analysis of *Tristanakkord* the tendency in reviews and secondary literature to highlight comparisons between Treichel and other contemporary German writers, most notably Martin Walser. The chapter argues that in *Tristanakkord* Treichel successfully challenges one-dimensional cultural globalization, without falling into a conservative appeal to the notion of a supposedly authentic German *Heimat* as an antidote to the rootlessness of modern society. In this he is most obviously different from Martin Walser. Rhys Williams then examines *Der irdische Amor*, identifying the significance of Caravaggio as a topic of study for the protagonist Albert and for the novel as a whole, while analysing the mechanics of Treichel's comic vision. As in previous volumes, the final chapter comprises a detailed bibliography.

Abbreviations

Throughout the current volume, the quotations from primary texts by Hans-Ulrich Treichel, unless otherwise indicated, will be followed by one of the abbreviations listed below and the relevant page number(s) in parentheses. The editions referred to are those most widely available.

VLS *Von Leib und Seele* (Frankfurt am Main, Suhrkamp, 1998).

V *Der Verlorene* (Frankfurt am Main, Suhrkamp, 1999).

H *Heimatkunde oder Alles ist heiter und edel* (Frankfurt am Main, Suhrkamp, 2000).

T *Tristanakkord* (Frankfurt am Main, Suhrkamp, 2000).

EA *Der Entwurf des Autors. Frankfurter Poetikvorlesungen* (Frankfurt am Main, Suhrkamp, 2000).

iA *Der irdische Amor* (Frankfurt am Main, Suhrkamp, 2002).

1

Gedichte

HANS-ULRICH TREICHEL

An mich selbst

Ich grüße dich, alter Berliner,
echt aus Westfalen, vielmals umgezogener,
windiger Weddinger, kreuzbraver Kreuzberger,
immer kohlenbeheizter, frierender, fluchender
Außenklonutzer, wie oft hast du
auf dem Treppenabsatz kehrt gemacht,
wie selten hast du die Treppe gekehrt,
ich winke dir zu, aus dem blühenden Lankwitz,
wo du jetzt prächtige Mieten bezahlst,
den Windhund ausführst auf der Dachterrasse,
Funken sprühst vor dem Fernseher, alter
Anarcho, alter Parkettfeger, du.

Rüdesheimer Platz

Ich setze mich unter den Baum.
Privatbesitz: eine Hundertschaft
Drosseln hat ihn erobert. Ich rücke
den Drahtstuhl neben den Brunnen, studiere
das Wasser, es zittert wie Seidenpapier.
Ich schließe die Augen, lausche.
Mein Atem geht hoffnungslos schnell.

Südraum Leipzig

Die Braunkohle stand wie der Hopfen so hoch.
Dann kam die Grube, weit wie die Nordsee.
Bagger und Bänder zitterten leise, Eisen
rieb Eisen. Gleich wird geflutet, rief der Mann
von der Umweltbehörde. Über die Halde rannte
ein Rebhuhn. Ich weiß nicht wohin.

Tagesbilanz

Der Abendhimmel über mir,
die Magensäure in mir,
das Flattern der Augenlider,
ich schließe den Vorhang,
notiere meine Werte:
Angstindex leicht sinkend,
Bitterstoffe konstant.

Ich, der Vertriebene

Hier bin ich wieder, ich,
der Vertriebene, doch diesmal
mit dem Gesicht nach unten,
ins Gras gedrückt, in die
schwarze westfälische Erde,
in den staubigen Grunewaldsand.
Irgendwo müsst ihr doch sein,
Urahnen, ihr, meine Wurzeln,
die Tante mit Hut, der Onkel
mit Koffer, der Opa aus Sonstwo,
die rissige Holzbank, das Pferd.
Farne, Libellen und Kiesel,
warum redet ihr nicht?

In Weimar im Winter

Dem Bettler im Garten fehlen
zwei Mark, für den Zug nach Apolda,
ich muß nach Apolda, heißt die Parole,
wer wollte da knausern, in Weimar,
im Winter, am Ufer der Ilm, auf dem
Kiesweg des Meisters, wer gäbe da nichts,
wo Christiane, die Gute, Quecken
ausstreute, auch wenn wir uns sanftere
Witterung wünschten, gelbere Blumen,
lichtere Farben, und, lieber Bettler,
ein edleres Ziel.

Biographie

Es war nicht Mühsal gewesen,
nicht Plage, es dauerte nicht
neunzig und auch keine siebzig
Jahr, es war nicht köstlich gewesen,
auch nicht von Übel, da war nur
manchmal ein Schmerz in den Adern,
ein Pochen im Schädel, der Himmel
riß nicht auf, der Teppich blieb
von der Sintflut verschont.

Anflug Kiew

Unter mir der Fluß
mit dem rollenden Namen,
er rollte durch meine Kindheit,
entsprang im Mund des Vaters,
der das Schilf schnitt am Ufer,
der den Stör fing, den Lachs,
der den weißen ukrainischen Himmel
mit schwäbischer Gründlichkeit
pflügte, Zäune zog durch die Wildnis,
nach zwei Kriegen noch immer
herumtrug im Mund und unter der
Zunge die Geräusche des Flusses,
der noch immer den Pflug zog
durch Nebel und Sumpf.

Teiresias

Was wollt ihr, ich habe nur meine
verschorften Pupillen. Ich sage euch nur,
daß Spatzen und Scherben zu niemandem sprechen,
der Wind heult wie Wind, der Regen ist Wasser.
Was wollt ihr, da ist nichts, nur dieses Jucken
hinter den Lidern, die grindige Netzhaut,
der Türspalt voll Licht.

2

Hans-Ulrich Treichel: Outline Biography

DAVID BASKER

1952   Hans-Ulrich Treichel was born on 12 August in Versmold in Westphalia.
1979   Publication of the poetry anthology *Ein Restposten der Zukunft*.
1981   Treichel received the Arbeitsstipendium des Berliner Senats.
1981–2 Treichel worked as a German language Lektor at the University of Salerno in Italy.
1982   Publication of the poetry anthology *Tarantella*.
1984   Treichel received his doctorate for *Fragment ohne Ende. Eine Studie zum Werk Wolfgang Koeppens*, also published in 1984.
1984–5 Treichel taught at the Scuola Normale Superiore in Pisa in Italy.
1985   Treichel received the Leonce-und-Lena-Preis der Stadt Darmstadt.
       Academic post in modern German literature at the Freie Universität in Berlin (until 1991).
1986   Publication of the poetry anthology *Liebe Not*.
       Publication of Wolfgang Koeppen's *Gesammelte Werke*, of which Treichel was co-editor.
1988   Stipendiary guest of the Villa Massimo in Rome.
1990   Publication of the poetry anthology *Seit Tagen kein Wunder*.
1992   Publication of the collection of prose writing *Von Leib und Seele. Berichte*.
1993   *Habilitation* on aspects of modernist literature (see 1995 below).
       Treichel received the Förderpreis zum Bremer Literaturpreis for the book *Von Leib und* Seele.
1994   Publication of the poetry anthology *Der einzige Gast*.

1995 Treichel became Professor at the Deutsche Literaturinstitut at the University of Leipzig.
Publication of Treichel's *Habilitationsschrift* as *Auslöschungsverfahren. Exemplarische Untersuchungen zur Literatur und Poetik der Moderne.*
Publication of *Wolfgang Koeppen: Einer der schreibt. Gespräche und Interview*, edited and with a foreword by Treichel.

1996 Publication of the collection of prose writing *Heimatkunde oder Alles ist heiter und edel. Besichtigungen.*

1998 Publication of Treichel's first novel, *Der Verlorene.*

2000 Publication of Treichel's second novel, *Tristanakkord*, and of the collection *Über die Schrift hinaus. Essays zur Literatur.*
Treichel invited to deliver the Frankfurter Poetik-Vorlesungen. Published as *Der Entwurf des Autors.*

2002 Publication of the novel *Der irdische Amor.*
Publication of a collection of Treichel's previously published poems as *Gespräch unter Bäumen. Gesammelte Gedichte.*

2003 Treichel awarded the Margarete-Schrader-Preis für Literatur and the Annette-von-Droste-Hülshoff-Preis.

3

»Leseerfahrungen sind Lebenserfahrungen«: Gespräch mit Hans-Ulrich Treichel

RHYS W. WILLIAMS

RWW: Ich möchte mit den Leseerfahrungen der Kindheit, mit den ersten literarischen Erlebnissen anfangen. Was für Bücher haben Sie als Kind gelesen?

H-UT: Da gab es keine besonderen Leseerlebnisse, ich bin nicht literarisch sozialisiert. Mir wurde zum Einschlafen nicht Thomas Mann vorgelesen, und auch nicht Grimms Märchen. Ich bin in einem protestantischen Elternhaus aufgewachsen, mit einem strengen Arbeitsethos, wo es neben der Bibel nicht viele Bücher gab. Insofern hatte ich bis zur Pubertät, bevor ich selber entscheiden konnte, keine wirklich literarischen Leseerlebnisse. Bis dahin waren die einzige Quelle meiner Bildung die sogenannten Illustrierten Klassiker, eine Heftchenreihe, die im elterlichen Geschäft verkauft wurde. Durch die *Illustrierten Klassiker* habe ich, ohne zu wissen, daß es um Literatur ging, *King Lear*, *Macbeth* oder auch *Die Schatzinsel* kennen gelernt. Ich habe dann später, als ich den Werken in Buchform begegnet bin, Wiedererkennungseffekte gehabt. Aber das ist natürlich keine literarische Bildung gewesen.

RWW: Kam die Bildung dann von der Schule her?

H-UT: Die Schule war anfangs auch nicht so wichtig. Das Lesen war eine Zeitlang sogar gegen die Schule gerichtet, und natürlich auch gegen meinen Lebensraum, die westfälische Provinz. In der Pubertät hat eine Suchbewegung eingesetzt, wie das ja oft der Fall ist, und plötzlich waren Lektüreinteressen da. Ich und einige Freunde haben uns allerdings einer Überforderung ausgesetzt, indem wir gleich Sartre, Marcuse und andere schwierige philosophische oder auch literarische Texte gelesen haben. Ich weiß, daß ich einige Bücher zu früh gelesen habe. Camus zum Beispiel: Ich erinnere mich, daß ich *Die Pest* gelesen habe, ohne das

Gespräch mit Hans-Ulrich Treichel

Buch wirklich zu verstehen oder eine Beziehung zu dem Text aufbauen zu können. Und ich habe später zu meinem Bedauern feststellen müssen, daß das Verhältnis zu zu früh gelesenen Büchern immer ein gespanntes, irritiertes bleibt. Als habe man für immer die Chance zu einer angemessenen Lektüre vertan, wenn man ein Buch einmal vor der Zeit aufgeschlagen hat. Daneben hat auch die Musik eine große Rolle gespielt, das Musikhören vor allen Dingen, das nicht wirklich weiter geführt, nicht zur Musik hin und schon gar nicht zu einem künstlerisch aktiven Zustand. Bloß zu der Einbildung, aktiv zu sein. Aber das gehört zu pubertären oder adoleszenten Entwicklungsphasen wahrscheinlich dazu, daß man das Musikhören, das zuweilen geradezu exzessive Plattenhören als kunstausübenden Zustand begreift. Was natürlich eine Illusion ist, wenn man da nur die Luftgitarre spielt, sonst nichts. In einem Text Goethes über den Dilettantismus gibt es so eine Bemerkung, daß der Dilettant auf lebhafte Weise Wirkungen erleidet und darum glaubt, mit diesen Wirkungen wirken zu können. Ich kann mich im nachhinein mit dieser Diagnose sehr gut identifizieren.

RWW: Kann man Ihre Kindheit als glücklich bezeichnen?

H-UT: Ich habe meine Kindheit in den Frankfurter Poetikvorlesungen thematisiert, unter der Überschrift 'Lektionen der Leere'. Ich hätte dies auch unter dem Stichwort 'Jenseits von Glück und Unglück' tun können, denn beides trifft zu. Ich kann nicht behaupten, daß meine Kindheit besonders schön war, sie war aber auch nicht besonders schlimm. Es war eher ein leerer und auch dumpfer Zustand, der irgendwann vergangen ist. Wobei man das wiederum auch als schlimm empfinden kann, so eine kindheitslose Kindheit in einer weltlosen, erfahrungsleeren Provinz und in einem vom Krieg und von der Flucht traumatisierten Elternhaus. Aber ich habe mir zumindest vorgenommen, es nicht so schlimm zu finden.

RWW: Und diese Leere, wann haben Sie zum ersten Mal versucht, diese Leere mit eigener Literatur aufzufüllen?

H-UT: In der Pubertät habe ich nicht geschrieben. Als Kind habe ich Märchen geschrieben, aber das ist schnell weg gewesen. Das aktive Schreiben ist erst während des Germanistikstudiums passiert.

RWW: Als Korrektur, sozusagen?

H-UT: Ja, ich glaube, die Entscheidung Germanistik zu studieren war schon eine Entscheidung, die Nähe der Literatur zu suchen. In dem Bestreben, Literatur zu analysieren, verbirgt sich womöglich der Wunsch, das Geheimnis der literarischen Produktivität zu entdecken, herauszubekommen, wie Literatur entsteht und gemacht wird – das Produktionsgeheimnis zu lüften, nicht nur das Bedeutungsgeheimnis. Als ich studiert habe – ich habe 1971/72 angefangen – war das Studium sehr literatursoziologisch. Ich habe erst mal jahrelang Theorie gelesen, Kurse über das Marxsche Kapital besucht, mich mit der sogenanten ursprünglichen Akkumulation beschäftigt, dem Fetischcharakter der Ware, dem falschen Bewußtsein und der Ideologiekritik. Ich habe Lukács, Bloch, Benjamin, Adorno gelesen, bevor ich literarische Texte wirklich wahrgenommen habe. Wobei ich es gern gemacht habe, das Theoriestudium, zeitweise auch mit wirklicher Begeisterung. Gleichwohl hat sich irgendwann während des Studiums das Gefühl eingestellt, daß dies, der analytische Zugriff, nicht alles war, was ich von der Literatur und wohl auch von mir selbst wollte. In den letzten Studiensemestern – 1975, 1976 – habe ich dann angefangen, eigene Sachen zu schreiben. Also relativ spät eigentlich. Mein erster Gedichtband ist 1979 erschienen. Es ist für einen Studenten der Literatur natürlich schwer, sich angesichts des Kanons nun hinzusetzen und eigene Verse zu schreiben. Zumal dieser Kanon ja in der Germanistischen Bibliothek der Freien Universität sozusagen körperlich vor mir und um mich herum stand. Man braucht also ein ziemliches Selbstbewußtsein, um als Germanistikstudent mit dem Schreiben zu beginnen. Oder aber man mußte einer entsprechenden inneren Notsituation ausgesetzt sein, die einen wider alle Vernunft zum Schreiben zwingt.

RWW: In den Gedichten hört man gewisse Stimmen: Bertolt Brecht und vielleicht Gottfried Benn. Gab es Vorbilder in der Lyrik?

H-UT: Das sind zwei wichtige Namen. Wobei Benn mir eher unterlaufen ist, weil ich, und natürlich nicht nur ich, sehr viele politische Vorbehalte gegen Benn hatte. Benn war mir sehr fern, gedanklich. Aber aus dieser Ferne hat sich dann doch wiederum eine Nähe ergeben, und dafür verantwortlich war wohl diese spezielle Schwermut in Benns Gedichten. Aber es mögen auch noch andere Dinge dabei ein Rolle spielen. So haben mich gewisse Benn-Fotografien immer an meinen Vater erinnert – der Hut, der Mantel, die Krawatte, die schwarzen Lederschuhe, dieser ganze eingezwängte, verpackte Herrenstil. Das war mir fremd und nahe zugleich. Brecht war mir nicht fremd. Was natürlich auch auf einem Mißverständnis beruht. Aber er war gleich der Hausheilige, schon relativ früh. Er war sozusagen der Dichter der Jugend. Und mit ihm die Brecht-Schule der deutschen Gegenwartslyrik – Enzensberger vor allem – die aber auch eine Benn-Schule war, nur war dies erst auf den zweiten Blick zu entdecken. Und dann gab es so Seitentriebe des Interesses, wie Lorca und Alberti, oder Ungaretti und Saba. Überhaupt spanische und italienische Lyriker des zwanzigsten Jahrhunderts.

RWW: Zuerst kam der Gedichtband *Ein Restposten der Zukunft*, dann *Tarantella*, und dann 1986 *Liebe Not*.

H-UT: Ja, *Liebe Not* war der dritte Gedichtband und der erste Band bei Suhrkamp.

RWW: Und wie kam es dazu? Haben Sie einfach den Gedichtband an den Suhrkamp Verlag geschickt?

H-UT: Nein, ich hatte den zweiten Band 1982 veröffentlicht. Beide Verlage, bei denen ich meine ersten zwei Bücher veröffentlicht hatte, waren Kleinverlage, Nebenerwerbsbetriebe in gewisser Weise. Von denen nur noch einer und der wohl auch nur noch pro forma existiert. Ich habe dann einen dritten Band geschrieben. Es gab sogar schon die Druckfahnen, das Buch sollte bei meinem zweiten Verlag erscheinen. Dann habe ich mich am Leonce-und-Lena-Preiswettbewerb beteiligt, einem relativ bekannten Lyrikwettbewerb für junge Autoren. Man schickt zwölf Gedichte hin, dann wird man mit einigen anderen Autoren zur Endausscheidung nach Darmstadt eingeladen. Das ist mir auch so gegangen. Ich habe dann erfreulicherweise gewonnen, und in der Jury war, neben Marcel Reich-Ranicki und Ernst Jandl, auch Elisabeth Borchers, selbst angesehene Lyrikerin und zugleich Lektorin des Suhrkamp Verlags. Sie hat mich gefragt, ob ich mehr als diese zwölf Gedichte habe. Ich hatte ja ein ganzes Manuskript und habe es ihr dann geschickt. Zum Bedauern meines damaligen Verlegers Harald Schmid, der aber großzügig war und mich schließlich noch bestärkte, den Verlagswechsel vorzunehmen. Wenn man anfängt, aus einem kleinen Verlag kommt oder nicht einmal das, dann bedarf es eben irgend eines Hebels, damit ein größerer Verlag aufmerksam wird. Für mich war der Leonce-und-Lena-Preis dieser Hebel. Hätte ich mein Manuskript aus der völligen Anonymität heraus an den Verlag geschickt, wäre es möglicherweise übersehen worden, obwohl ich andererseits glaube, daß ein gutes Manuskript immer seinen Verlag finden wird.

RWW: Die Gedichte sind alle sehr knapp, Sie schreiben keine langen Gedichte. Es sind Momentaufnahmen, Stimmungsbilder, Alltagssituationen, die aber nicht im bloßen Alltag verbleiben, sondern immer wieder auch auf literarische Vorbilder verweisen und mit literarischen Anspielungen arbeiten. Man merkt eine gewisse literarhistorische Bildung und wie wichtig Ihnen die Literatur ist.

H-UT: Ich hoffe aber, daß es keine Bildungsgedichte sind. Doch meine Überzeugung ist, daß Leseerfahrungen Lebenserfahrungen sind. Das hat auch den Effekt, daß sich dann Lektüreerfahrungen in Gedichten ebenso niederschlagen können wie andere persönliche Erfahrungen auch, das Reisen beispielsweise oder ein Besuch im Schwimmbad. Wobei mit lyrisch verarbeiteten Lektüreerfahrungen natürlich nicht das bloße Zitieren von Büchern oder Autoren gemeint ist, sondern der lyrische Bezug auf literarische Kontexte, zu denen Dichterbiographien ebenso gehören können wie mythologische Figuren oder Landschaften und Städte. Man nehme nur Rom oder Venedig beispielsweise. Wer heute ein Rom- oder Venediggedicht schreibt, und sei es ein noch so persönlich gemeintes Reisegedicht, der reagiert *nolens volens* auf einen vorgegebenen literarischen Kontext. Natürlich bin ich mir bewußt, daß man immer ein Stück eigener Deutung hinzutut, wenn man sich auf diese Weise auf den Kanon bezieht. Aber das macht schließlich den Reiz des Spielens und Anspielens aus.

RWW: Ich möchte jetzt auf die Germanistik zurückkommen. Sie haben über Wolfgang Koeppen promoviert und die Ausgabe seiner Gesammelten Werke mitherausgegeben. Wie sind Sie auf Koeppen als Thema gekommen?

H-UT: Ich habe Koeppen in Seminaren kennengelernt, während des Studiums. Ich kannte ihn vorher nicht. Mein Doktorvater, Klaus Scherpe, hatte sich auch schon mit Koeppen beschäftigt, und es war in einem seiner Seminare, wo wir *Tauben im Gras* gelesen haben. Mein Interesse für Koeppen war also ein echter Lehrerfolg der Universität! Nach *Tauben im Gras* habe ich Koeppens andere Bücher gelesen und das Werk insgesamt für mich entdeckt. Wobei es mit den persönlichen Entdeckungen und Vorlieben ja zumeist so ist, daß man damit oft genug auf etwas reagiert, was bereits in der Luft liegt. Und Koeppens Wiederentdeckung lag in den siebziger Jahren in der Luft. 1976 erschien *Jugend* bei Suhrkamp, und bei dieser Gelegenheit wurde das ganze Werk noch mal kommentiert. *Jugend* war zwar nicht der große Roman, auf den die Öffentlichkeit so lange schon, im Grunde seit Mitte der fünfziger Jahre, gewartet hatte. Aber es war immerhin ein geschlossener erzählerischer Text, auch wenn er sich einer fragmentarischen Kompositionsweise verdankt und in Schüben entstanden ist. In dieser Zeit lebten auch die Diskussionen um den »Schweiger Koeppen« und um den »Fall Koeppen« wieder auf. Reich-Ranicki beispielsweise hat sich fortlaufend eingeschaltet und Koeppen und *Jugend* stark unterstützt. Diese Resonanzen von Außen haben natürlich auch eine Rolle bei meinem Interesse gespielt. Aber letztlich war natürlich das Leseerlebnis das entscheidende, und für mich war *Tauben im Gras* eines der spannendsten Bücher über die fünfziger Jahre, das sich zugleich aber durch große Gegenwärtigkeit auszeichnete.

RWW: Haben Sie darin Ihre eigene Kindheit wiederentdeckt?

H-UT: Nein, überhaupt nicht. Ich habe darin nichts gefunden, was ich unmittelbar auf mich hätte beziehen können. Nichts von meinen eigenen fünfziger Jahren. Meine Koeppen-Lektüre war keine identifikatorische Lektüre. Dieser Kosmos in München, von dem Koeppen erzählt, war nicht mit den leeren Feldwegen in Ostwestfalen zu vergleichen. Identifikatorisch habe ich allenfalls den speziellen Koeppen-Ton wahrgenommen, die Musikalität der Sprache, das Tempo und die Dynamik des Textes und seine besondere Melancholie. Wobei mich speziell in *Tauben im Gras* natürlich auch die scheiternde Schriftstellerfigur des Philip interessiert hat, in der ja auch Züge des Autors aufscheinen.

RWW: Sie sind immer noch Germanist, Sie beschäftigen sich immer noch mit der deutschen Literatur. Welche anderen Autoren sind für Sie wichtig?

H-UT: Ich habe meine Habilitationsschrift über ein Thema der literarischen Moderne geschrieben, über das Motiv und das Verfahren der Auslöschung. Genauer: Über Auslöschung als Motiv und Verfahren. Wichtig ist beispielsweise Robert Walser für mich geworden, aber auch Ernst Jünger, obwohl er mir in jeder Beziehung fremd war und ist. Sowohl im politischen als auch im habituellen Sinne. Was Jünger angeht, da habe ich natürlich auch schon, bevor ich ihn gelesen habe, ein festes Bild gehabt: der soldatische, rechte Autor. Ich habe dann mehr durch Zufall *Siebzig verweht I*, den ersten Band der späten Tagebücher, gelesen, und ich habe während der Lektüre festgestellt, daß das Buch alle meine Vorurteile bestätigt. Aber ich mußte zugleich feststellen, daß ich trotzdem immer weiter gelesen habe. Ich habe am Ende das ganze umfangreiche Buch gelesen, es war auf einer Sizilienreise, woran ich mich gut erinnere, und ich war auf eine eigentümliche Weise fasziniert von dieser mir doch völlig fernliegenden Welthaltung und Lebensführung, die Jünger verkörpert: so studienrätlich latinisierend bildungsbewußt, dann dieses mineralogische, pflanzenkundliche und entomologische Interesse, das Gärtnern und Insektensammeln, dazwischen immer wieder soldatische Korrespondenzpartner, Offiziere, alte Kameraden, alles sehr merkwürdig eigentlich. Für Insekten beispielsweise hatte ich mich nie interessiert. Und für Steine auch nicht allzu sehr. Gleichwohl war da etwas, was mich verführt hat, weiterzulesen. Und das hat mir dann doch zu denken gegeben. So habe ich angefangen, mich mit Jünger zu beschäftigen und gelegentlich auch über ihn zu schreiben. Ich wollte herausbekommen, warum ich ihn lese.

RWW: Dann sind drei Gedichtbände – *Liebe Not*, *Set Tagen, kein Wunder*, und *Der einzige Gast* – bei Suhrkamp erschienen.

H-UT: Ja, aber es hat sich die erste Prosa, der Band *Von Leib und Seele*, der 1992 erschienen ist, dazwischengeschoben.

RWW: War das für Sie schwierig, auf Prosa umzusteigen, oder war da schon immer eine Anziehung?

H-UT: Lange Zeit eigentlich nicht. Ich bin zum Gedicht gekommen, indem ich als Student Tagebuch geschrieben habe. Allerdings mußte ich die Erfahrung machen, daß das Tagebuchschreiben einerseits zur Geschichte und zum Erzählen drängte, daß ich aber andererseits immer dann, wenn ich mehr als einen Absatz schrieb und sich der Eintrag zu einer Geschichte auszuweiten begann, ins Stocken geriet. Es war, als ob eine rote Warnlampe angehen würde. Als ob ich mir selbst zurufen würde: Bitte nicht weiter schreiben, es könnte etwas Verborgenes ausgeplaudert werden! Ich habe dann dieses Schreibverbot, diese Erzählstörung insofern für mich fruchtbar zu machen versucht, indem ich zur Kurzform griff, die Zeilen abbrach – so daß aus den Tagebucheinträgen am Ende keine Anfänge von Erzählungen wurden, sondern erste und noch ziemlich prosaische Alltagsgedichte. Aber das war die Form, die es mir überhaupt möglich machte, zu schreiben, und aus der ich dann meine weiteren lyrischen Texte heraus entwickeln konnte. Ich habe dann längere Zeit nur Gedichte geschrieben, und dann, nachdem drei oder vier Gedichtbände entstanden waren und ein ziemliches Stück Lebenszeit vergangen war, doch gespürt, daß ich bestimmte Dinge in der Gattung Lyrik nicht aussprechen kann, sie nun aber aussprechen und vor allem erzählen möchte. Denn die besondere Möglichkeit der Lyrik, ihre Kürze und Verschwiegenheit, ist natürlich auch ihre Grenze. Diese Grenze war der Grund, es mit Prosa zu versuchen – obwohl ich einen riesigen Respekt vor Prosaautoren hatte. Da ich nur mit Gedichten, also kleinen Texteinheiten gearbeitet hatte, war es mir unvorstellbar, wie man einen Stoff so lange festhalten kann, wie es die Romanautoren tun. Aber ich habe dann in der Villa Massimo eine gute Gelegenheit gefunden, mich als Prosaautor zu erproben.

RWW: Man hat das Gefühl, wenn man *Von Leib und Seele* liest, daß Humor eine größere Rolle in der Prosa spielt als in den Gedichten. Ich denke an die Geschichte von dem jungen Mann, der nach Salerno geht und versucht, die Universität zu finden. Das sind sehr humorvolle Geschichten. Humor ist plötzlich eine andere Art, mit der Welt umzugehen. Sehen Sie das auch so?

H-UT: Ja, das stimmt, die Gedichte sind stärker von Melancholie und Schwermut geprägt. In meiner spontanen Alltagserfahrung war ein humorvoller, ironischer oder auch sarkastischer Blick auf die Welt sicher schon immer da. Aber eben nicht als erzählerische oder gar formgebende Haltung. Denn diesen Blick, diesen Einstellungswinkel zur Welt kann man sich nicht vornehmen. Ich jedenfalls kann es nicht. Er muß sich von selbst, spontan ergeben. Aus dem eigenen Temperament heraus. So habe ich auch nie mit dem Vorsatz geschrieben: ich mache das jetzt komisch oder ironisch. Die Ironie ergibt sich für mich sozusagen notwendigerweise, weil sie mir auch lebensnotwendig erscheint. Sie nimmt Gepäck von den Schultern, Existenzlast, was ich als befreiend empfinde.

RWW: Ja, das hat auch eine befreiende Wirkung auf den Leser.

H-UT: Wobei es auch eine Ironie des Materials und Perspektive gibt. Eine Ironie oder Komik, die Effekt eines speziellen erzählerischen Blickes und Verfahrens ist. Zumindest habe ich oft genug beim Schreiben nicht das Gefühl, daß es jetzt komisch ist, was da auf den Seiten vor mir geschieht. Im Nachhinein aber stelle ich es dann fest. Und ich denke, daß eine bestimmte Form der Wahrnehmung, eine gewisse zwanghafte Genauigkeit oder ein starres Fixieren der Dinge einen komischen Effekt schaffen kann, der anfangs gar nicht beabsichtigt ist.

RWW: Die Erzählungen in *Von Leib und Seele* enthalten aber auch Begegnungen mit der Familie. Diese Beschreibungen sind nicht so witzig. Kommen hier die bedrängenderen Probleme zum Vorschein?

H-UT: Ja, das ist möglich. Die Verstrickungen sind da größer, das Terrain unsicherer, der Boden unter den Füßen wankender, das Spielerische ist nicht so stark.

RWW: Nach *Von Leib und Seele* kam *Heimatkunde* ...

H-UT: Ja, das ist eigentlich eine Fortsetzung des ersten Prosabandes, es sind wiederum meist autobiographische Erzählungen und einige Reiseerzählungen. Und vielleicht auch Kapitel eines nicht geschriebenen Romans.

Gespräch mit Hans-Ulrich Treichel

RWW: ... und dann kam 1998 *Der Verlorene*.

H-UT: Das sieht ein wenig teleologisch aus: am Ende steht der Roman. Doch das ist gar nicht beabsichtigt gewesen. *Der Verlorene* sollte anfangs eine kürzere Erzählung über Familienfotos werden, das war das ursprüngliche Vorhaben. Ich war schon immer der Meinung, daß ich auf allen Familienfotos immer am schlechtesten von allen getroffen bin, oft nur halb zu sehen und manchmal auch fast gar nicht, nur mit einem Auge, einem Ohr oder einem Bein. Darüber wollte ich schreiben. Über diesen Komplex der Nichtanwesenheit oder der bloß fragmentarischen Anwesenheit. Dann kam das Photo des verlorenen Bruders dazu. Und plötzlich hatte ich eine Geschichte, die über das Fotomotiv weit hinausging.

RWW: Es gibt frühere Gedichte über Fotoalben, die man erst völlig verstehen kann, wenn man den *Verlorenen* gelesen hat.

H-UT: Ja, *Der Verlorene* gibt gewissermaßen die Rahmenbedingungen und Begleitumstände an.

RWW: *Der Verlorene* hat eine sehr große öffentliche Wirkung gehabt. Ich bin nicht sehr überzeugt von der Rezeption des Buches, weil man es als repräsentativ für eine Generation von Deutschen gedeutet hat: Die Deutschen sind jetzt bereit, sich als Opfer darzustellen. Man versucht Bernhard Schlinks *Der Vorleser* mit Ihrem Buch zusammenzubringen, was ich auch nicht besonders überzeugend finde.

H-UT: Ich auch nicht. Dies aber ganz unabhängig von meiner Wertschätzung des *Vorlesers*. Doch handelt es sich bei den beiden Büchern um zwei ganz unterschiedliche Erzählverfahren, denke ich.

RWW: Meines Erachtens ist *Der Verlorene* eher mit dem Ich-Erzähler beschäftigt, als mit dem Verlorenen.

H-UT: Ich würde es, um dieses Wort auch einmal zu sagen, dialektisch sehen. Der Ich-Erzähler ist auch ein Verlorener. Und das Buch erzählt unter anderem die Geschichte eines Anwesenden, der immer abwesender wird, und eines Abwesenden, der immer anwesender wird. Aber um noch einmal auf den *Vorleser* zurückzukommen. Ich habe festgestellt, daß man noch ein drittes Buch in diese Reihe gestellt hat, und zwar Marcel Beyers *Flughunde*. Und natürlich ist auch das ein wohl hervorragender, aber gänzlich anders erzählter Text.

RWW: Es hat seit *Die Blechtrommel* viele Bücher gegeben, die den Nationalsozialismus thematisierten. Was ist an Ihrem Buch neu?

H-UT: Das Neue ist möglicherweise, daß jetzt Autoren, die in den fünfziger oder sogar den sechziger Jahren geboren sind, erneut auf die Wirkung des Nationalsozialismus für ihr eigenes Leben stoßen und dieser Wirkung nun nachspüren. Für mich selbst scheint das Besondere, das ich, obwohl ich 1952 geboren und damit kein echtes Nachkriegskind und schon gar kein Kriegskind bin, in meiner Biographie plötzlich etwas entdecke, was mich unmittelbar an die Kriegszeit und an die Kriegsfolgen anbindet. Es gibt in der Traumaforschung den Begriff der transgenerationellen Traumatisierung, und ich bemerke, daß die Traumatisierung der Elterngeneration, also die Erfahrung von Krieg, Flucht und Verfolgung, mir nicht nur in der Kindheit mitgegeben wurde, sondern mich auch über einen langen Zeitraum noch erreicht. *Der Verlorene* erzählt von dieser Traumatisierung. Wobei es für mich selbst symptomatisch ist, daß ich dieses Buch erst in den neunziger Jahren geschrieben habe und nicht etwa zehn oder fünfzehn Jahre früher, was ja vom Lebensalter her durchaus möglich gewesen wäre. Insofern stellt das Buch eine sehr späte Reaktion eines Nachgeborenen auf ein nicht sehr oft erzähltes Erleiden dar.

RWW: Es geht über die Wirkungen der Wirkungen?

H-UT: Ja, genau. Ich habe das nicht mit dem Bewußtsein geschrieben, daß ich jetzt recherchiere, Historie ausgrabe, mich über Dokumente und Fotoalben beuge und dabei zurückversetze, sondern ich habe das aus einem starken Gegenwartsgefühl heraus geschrieben. Irgend etwas muß es sozusagen ermöglicht oder auch erzwungen haben, daß ich plötzlich in meiner Gegenwart Mitte der neunziger Jahre eine starke Nachwirkung des Fluchtereignisses thematisiere.

RWW: Haben Sie viel von Ihren Eltern über diese Ereignisse gehört?

H-UT: Fast nichts. Ich habe nur das Nicht-Erzählen-Können verspürt. Jede Frage endete nach zwei oder drei Sätzen mit Schweigen, mit Ablenkungen oder mit Tränen. »Ach, das war schrecklich, Junge«. Das Trauma war natürlich in der Familie präsent, aber als Schweigen. Und daneben regierte der Vorsatz, sich »eine Existenz aufzubauen«. Das war eine feste Wendung, der Vater hatte sich ja auch schon die dritte Existenz aufgebaut. Das wollte er an die Kinder weitergeben. Das ist natürlich eine Haltung, die aus großen Verlust- und Angsterfahrungen resultiert. Aber diese Erfahrungen selbst wurden nicht erzählt.

RWW: Haben Sie dann den Zwang ererbt, von diesen Erfahrungen zu erzählen?

H-UT: Ja, vielleicht. Das hat für mich einen späten therapeutischen Effekt. Ich habe die Wirkung einer traumatischen Erfahrung gespürt, aber ich kenne die Erfahrung nicht, es gibt keine Erzählung dazu. Da ist ein Vakuum, eine Leerstelle. Diese fehlende Geschichte dann fiktional auszuerzählen, die Leerstelle zu füllen, das vertreibt den Phantomschmerz oder lindert ihn wenigstens. Man hat ja herausgefunden, daß Prothesen, die ja künstliche Ersetzungen sind, den Phantomschmerz vertreiben. Hinzu kommt die Erfahrung, schreibend mit der eigenen Biographie spielen zu können, ihr neue Gestalt zu geben und neue Erfahrungen zukommen zu lassen. Das kann eine Erfahrung von Souveränität sein. Man ist ja normalerweise seiner Biographie unterworfen: die eigene Lebensgeschichte hat man, ob man will oder nicht. Daß man sie umschreiben kann, das ist für einen Autor eine gute Erfahrung. Wobei umschreiben nicht einfach heißt, schlechte Erfahrungen durch gute ersetzen. Man kann auch Unglück hinzuerfinden, und sich dabei trotzdem erleichtert fühlen.

RWW: Wenn man *Tristanakkord* liest, hat man das Gefühl, daß ein biographisches Gespenst verbannt ist. Würden Sie da zustimmen?

H-UT: Vielleicht, aber das kann ich für mich gar nicht beurteilen. Vielleicht wachsen neue Gespenster heran!

RWW: Der Ton ist sehr spielerisch. Es geht zwar um einen jungen Mann, der Hemmungen hat, die aus seiner Kindheit im »Emsland«

herzurühren scheinen. Aber er setzt sich auf seine Weise doch immer durch. Und auf seine Weise scheint er seinem Widerpart, dem großen Komponisten, doch auch standhalten zu können. Man hat in der Figur des Komponisten eine Ähnlichkeit mit Hans Werner Henze gesehen. Hat ihre Zusammenarbeit mit ihm für den Roman eine Rolle gespielt?

H-UT: Ich habe als Librettist mit Henze zusammengearbeitet. Allerdings ist die wirkliche Geschichte eine ganz andere, als die, die im Buch erzählt wird. Gleichwohl gibt es so etwa wie einen motivischen Kern, der mir vertraut ist, eine Grundkonstellation, die darin besteht, daß ein junger, provinzieller und kulturell sehr unvollkommen sozialisierter Mensch in die Sphäre eines weltberühmten Künstlers tritt.

RWW: Wie ist es zu dieser Zusammenarbeit mit Henze gekommen?

H-UT: Das ist, wie so vieles im Leben, Zufall gewesen. Der Kontakt entstand über meinen Jugendfreund Jens Brockmeier, der Henzes Schriften beim Deutschen Taschenbuch Verlag herausgegeben hat. Ich habe Henze 1976 in London zum erstenmal getroffen, anläßlich der Uraufführung von *We come to the River* in Covent Garden. Wir sind dann in Kontakt geblieben und ich habe irgendwann begonnen, noch während des Studiums, mit ihm beziehungsweise seinen Schülern zu kooperieren und in seinen Musikwerkstätten mitzuarbeiten, in Montepulciano beispielsweise.

RWW: Das war Ende der siebziger Jahre?

H-UT: Ende der siebziger, Anfang der achtziger Jahre. Das fiel mit meinen eigenen ersten literarischen Arbeiten zusammen. Ich war gewissermaßen der einzige Schüler in Henzes Librettistenschule und bin so an die librettistische Tätigkeit herangeführt worden. Ich habe einige Projekte mit Kompositionsschülern von ihm gemacht: eine Brecht-Bearbeitung – *Das Badener Lehrstück vom Einverständnis* – dann *Aus der Zeit des Schweigens*, eine Art Kantate, ein Gedichtzyklus mit Gedichten über Rimbaud, und dann drei Opern für die Puppenbühne, die in Montepulciano uraufgeführt wurden. Irgendwann gab es die Anfrage, ob ich das Libretto für seine nächste Oper schreiben wolle. Das wurde dann die Oper *Das verratene Meer* nach dem Roman *Der Seemann, der die See verriet* von Yukio Mishima, die 1990 in Berlin an der Deutschen Oper uraufgeführt wurde. Danach haben wir *Venus und Adonis* gemacht und schließlich die *9. Symphonie*, eine Chorsymphonie, für die ich Texte nach Anna Seghers Roman *Das siebte Kreuz* geschrieben habe. Es ist also einiges entstanden und es verdankt sich wesentlich der engen persönlichen Zusammenarbeit mit dem Komponisten. Die Oper als Gattung war mir immer relativ fremd, ich bin mit Popmusik aufgewachsen, die Heroen meiner Jugend waren keine Tenöre. Aber durch die Arbeit als Librettist und gewissermaßen von Produktionsstandpunkt aus ist es für mich zu einem spannenden und fruchtbaren Prozeß geworden, mich der Oper anzunähern.

RWW: Ganz am Ende von *Tristanakkord* erscheint eine Frau. Das ist eine sehr ungewöhnliche Erscheinung in Ihrem Werk. Frauen sind wohl in ihrer Abwesenheit in den Gedichten da, aber in der Prosa spielen Frauenfiguren keine große Rolle.

H-UT: Abgesehen von der Figur der Mutter im *Verlorenen*. Sie ist zwar leidend und traumatisiert, aber für mich ist sie eine sehr wichtige und gegenwärtige Figur. Die Frau als Geliebte allerdings, da haben Sie recht, spielt in der Prosa bisher keine große Rolle. Als begehrte spielt sie allerdings schon eine Rolle. Im *Tristanakkord* heißt sie Mary, ist eine junge Amerikanerin und taucht schon vor dem Ende des Romans einmal kurz auf. Am Schluß gibt es dann so eine Art Voyeurismus-Szene, man könnte es auch eine Aktaion-und-Diana-Szene nennen. Nur daß die Aktaionquelle nicht in Boötien liegt, sondern ein Swimmingpool ist in einer süditalienischen Villa. Hier erblicken sowohl Georg, der Protagonist des Romans, wie auch Steven, der Assistent des Komponisten, die unbekleidete Mary. Und hier erstarren sie beide in ihrem unerlösten Begehren.

RWW: Drei Landschaften – Schottland, New York, Italien – sind wichtig in dem Roman, und ein wenig Berlin. Sind das für Sie exemplarische Landschaften?

H-UT: Zu Schottland habe ich keine große innere Beziehung, abgesehen von dem wunderbaren Lichtwechsel, den man dort erleben kann. Italien ist ja mein ganz spezielles Sehnsuchtsland der jungen Jahre gewesen, was nicht sehr originell ist, das gebe ich zu. Aber es ist eben auch ein einzigartiges Land. New York habe ich erst spät kennengelernt. Wobei es mit New York ein wenig wie mit Venedig ist. Diese Städte kennt man schon im voraus, sei es durch die Malerei, die Literatur oder den Film. Und es ist für einen Autor nicht leicht, sich diesen Städten literarisch anzunähern. Man kann nicht so tun, als ob alles neu sei, zum erstenmal gesehen. Man will aber auch die Stereotypen nicht reproduzieren, obwohl diese Stereotypen ja nicht immer ohne Wahrhaftigkeit sind. Darum kann man sie auch nicht einfach ignorieren. Man muß sich entschließen, mit ihnen zu arbeiten.

RWW: Sie waren sehr kurz in Swansea. Was hat hier einen besonderen Eindruck auf Sie gemacht?

H-UT: Die freundlichen Leute natürlich. Die guten Pubs. Die Wildpferde, die auf Golfplätzen grasen. Und das Klima, eine ganz überraschende Mischung von Norden und Süden, das meine Frau und ich während unserer täglichen Spaziergänge in und um Mumbles herum sehr genossen haben.

RWW: Das nächste Buch ist die Ausgabe der Frankfurter Poetikvorlesungen. Da haben Sie versucht, auf die eigene Produktion zurückzublicken, und auch auf die Landschaften und Orte, die ihnen wichtig waren, während der verschiedenen Lebensstadien.

H-UT: Als ich die Einladung zu den Poetikvorlesungen erhielt, habe ich mir natürlich erst einmal grundsätzlich überlegt, was ich dem Publikum, aber auch mir selbst zu sagen habe. Und was mich unter dem Stichwort 'Poetik' eigentlich interessiert. Und das war weniger das Technische, obwohl es mich auch interessiert. Aber ich wollte nicht die Frage nach der Machart und Herstellung der Texte in den Mittelpunkt rücken, und auch nicht allzu literaturtheoretisch oder philosophisch vorgehen. Hier gibt es ja bedeutende Vorgänger, Martin Walsers Poetikvorlesungen über Ironie und Selbstbewußtsein etwa, oder die Vorlesungen von Ingeborg Bachmann, mit der die Reihe der Frankfurter Vorlesungen vor vierzig Jahren ja begonnen hat. Es sind ja für Germanisten kanonische Werke inzwischen. Ich wollte mich mehr

Gespräch mit Hans-Ulrich Treichel

der Frage widmen, wie ich eigentlich zum Autor geworden bin. Die Herstellung des Autors sollte also das Thema sein, oder, so heißt das Buch ja auch, *Der Entwurf des Autors*. Eine poetologisch-biographische Erkundung also, an den eigenen Lebenslinien entlang. Wenn man sein eigenes Leben überschaut, dann stellt man ja fest, daß es so etwas wie Leitmotive gibt und Schlüsselszenen der Erfahrung, daß da eine gewisse Ordnung und Hierarchie der Themen und Stoffe existiert. Dazu gehören spezielle Kindheitserfahrungen, aber auch Orte und Landschaften und anderes mehr. Und natürlich drückt sich dies dann auch in der eigenen literarischen Arbeit aus und man kann von den Texten aus Rückschlüsse ziehen. In meinem Fall gehört zu diesen Schlüsselszenen und Leitmotiven natürlich die spezielle Leere der kindlichen Erfahrungen, das Erlebnis der ostwestfälischen Provinz und auch die Traumatisierung der Eltern und der Familienatmosphäre durch Krieg und Flucht. Wir haben anfangs darüber gesprochen. Und dazu gehört Berlin, vor allem das geteilte Berlin, das die Alternative zur Provinz darstellte, aber natürlich voller eigener Provinzialismen war. Dann das Reisen, diese beständige Suchbewegung, und eben auch der Süden, Italien und vor allem Rom als Ort der Sehnsucht und Enttäuschung zugleich.

RWW: Der Blick auf die eigene Biographie erinnert mich an Johnsons *Begleitumstände*.

H-UT: Ja, das ist vielleicht ähnlich. Vom Blick her. Nur daß die Umstände eben ganz andere sind.

RWW: Herr Treichel, ich bedanke mich herzlich für das Gespräch.

4

»Wenn du bedürftig bist, sinken deine Chancen«: Der Erzähler Hans-Ulrich Treichel zwischen Wirklichkeit und Vorstellung

STEPHAN REINHARDT

1

Am Anfang waren Fingerübungen – neben Gedichten auch Einübungen ins Prosaschreiben. Hans-Ulrich Treichel nannte seine 'Berichte' und 'Besichtigungen': *Von Leib und Seele* und *Heimatkunde oder Alles ist heiter und edel*. Besichtigt wurde und wird von Hans-Ulrich Treichel das Selbsterlebte, wurden und werden Situationen und Orte der eigenen Lebensgeschichte oder das von ihnen imaginativ Inspirierte: zum Beispiel 'Die Hausgeburt', die erste von zwölf Prosaskizzen:

> Das Zentrum des Hauses war die Küche, in der ich im Beisein des Hundes, einer schwarzen Labradorhündin, und einer Tante in der Rolle der Geburtshelferin an einem Augustnachmittag geboren wurde. Der Vater hatte auf einer Hausgeburt bestanden, da er das Geschäft nicht schließen und auch keine umständlichen Krankenhausbesuche machen wollte. (H, 7)

In der Regel kann kein Autor das in die Erinnerung zurückrufen, aber er hört dergleichen, wenn es später erzählt wird: Im von der Küche nur durch einen Vorhang getrennten 'Laden' verkaufte in der Erzählung 'Hausgeburt' der Vater Rauchwaren, Schnaps sowie Zeitungen und Zeitschriften (Treichels Vater war Großhändler in Tabakwaren). Und jedes Mal, wenn der geschäftstüchtige Vater bei den Wünschen der in den Laden kommenden Kunden nicht weiterwußte, steckte er den Kopf durch den Vorhang und »behelligte die von Wehen und Geburtsschmerzen geplagte Mutter mit seinen Fragen« (H, 8). Eine skurille, groteske, humoristische Situation – ein bizarres Grundmodell, das der Erzähler Hans-Ulrich Treichel in *Heimatkunde* in seinen kurzen Prosastücken etliche Male variiert und mit den Schauplätzen Berlin, Amrum, Stendal, Portugal und Venedig verbindet. Zu

Treichels erzählerischer Grundausstattung gehören dabei Instrumente wie Ironie und Spott. Mit ihnen stellt er Distanz her und mit ihrer Hilfe zeigt er seine Fähigkeit, Atmosphärisches psychologisch fein in Worte zu kleiden.

2
Besonders gut gelingt ihm das in seiner ersten großen Erzählung *Der Verlorene*. Treichels Icherzähler, ein pubertierender Dreizehn- oder Vierzehnjähriger, wächst in den Nachkriegsjahren in einer Familie heran, deren Atmosphäre »von Scham und Schuld« (V, 17) regelrecht vergiftet ist: Eine angesichts der in der NS-Zeit massenhaft aufgehäuften Schuld typisch deutsche Familien- situation. Ursache dieser lähmenden Bedrückung ist Arnold, der ältere Bruder. Er, klärt die Mutter den Icherzähler auf, sei in den letzten Kriegstagen, als sie und der Vater ihren ostpreußischen Bauernhof aus Furcht vor Vergeltung verlassen hatten, in ihren Armen verhungert – auf der Flucht vor den Russen. Dann korrigiert sie sich: Nein, nicht verhungert, sondern 'verlorengegangen'. Es sei so gewesen: Als die Russen ihren Flüchtlingstreck eingeholt und einige von ihnen sie und den Vater bedrängt hätten, habe sie ihren Arnold einer fremden Frau in die Arme gelegt. Gleich darauf sei diese Frau in der Menge verschwunden. Seither lastet dieser Verlust als tiefgehende seelische Verletzung auf der Familie. Der Icherzähler begreift, daß in seiner Familie der verlorene Bruder die Hauptrolle und er selbst nur eine Nebenrolle spielt.

Treichel stattet seine Hauptfigur mit einem psychologischen Grundgestus aus: Er gibt ihr den störrischen Blick dessen, der, weil ins zweite Glied zurückversetzt, gekränkt und ablehnend auf die geheime Konkurrenz des Bruders reagiert. Das traumatische Erlebnis der Eltern setzt sich so fort als seelische Belastung des Sohnes – ein Sachverhalt, den Treichel in eine scheinbar nüchtern- kühle Erzählperspektive und in einen Erzählfluß überträgt, der Distanz zum Schrecken herstellt – wiederum mit Hilfe seiner Ironie, Komik und seines leicht skurrilen Humors. Da ist die zu Besuch kommende Schwester des Vaters, die sich nur noch für die religiösen Wochenlosungen des Kirchenblatts interessiert und die, stellt der Vater das neue Statussymbol Fernseher an, dem Apparat stets den Rücken zukehrt, hält sie ihn doch für Teufelswerkzeug. Da erzählt ein Leichenwagenfahrer vom »absolut hygienisch« (V, 107) arbeitenden Bestattungswesen und von einem Krematoriumsdirektor, der zum Beweis des Todes eines der Toten-»Knöchelchen in den Mund genommen und darauf herumgebissen« (V, 106) habe. Da werden Schweineblut und Schweineköpfe regelmäßig ins Haus gebracht und von der Mutter zu den unterschiedlichsten Speisen, die fast das ganze Jahr über die Familie ernähren, verarbeitet: »Schweinebacke und Schweinezunge, Schweineohren und Schweineschnauze, Schweinekopfbrühe und Schweinekopfpaste« (V, 41).

Treichel beschreibt Familiengeschichte auch als Zeitgeschichte: Während die Mutter sich ihrem Schmerz über den verlorenen Sohn hingibt, kompensiert der Vater den Schmerz, indem er zum Gelingen des Wirtschaftswunders beiträgt. Doch so sehr sein Fleisch- und Wurstwarengroßhandel auch floriert, aller sich ansammelnder Reichtum vermag ihn nicht über den Verlust seines Sohnes Arnold hinwegzutrösten. Nur ein Babyfoto besitzt er noch von ihm. Dann die Überraschung: Das Rote Kreuz, über das sie Arnold suchen lassen, macht Hoffnung. Aber noch ehe die Familie Findelkind Nummer 2307 selbst zu Gesicht bekommt, werden Fingerabdrücke und Blutproben verglichen. Der Endbefund dann – erhoben in Heidelberg beim entscheidenden »anthropologisch-erbbiologischen Abstammungsgutachten« (V, 62–3) – schließt die Identität zwischen Findelkind und Arnold aus – zum Kummer der Eltern, zur Freude des Bruders.

Stoff und einige Motive der Erzählung *Der Verlorene* sind autobiographischen Ursprungs: Treichels älterer Bruder galt in der Familie als tot; erst vor ein paar Jahren erfuhr Treichel, daß er während der Flucht seiner Eltern 'verlorengegangen' war. Was die Eltern in der fiktiven Erzählform dem verbliebenen Sohn mitteilen, haben sie in der Realität verschwiegen. Mit eben diesem Verschweigen wird ein seelischer Mechanismus in Gang gesetzt, der tiefe Spuren hinterläßt: Indem die Eltern dem 'Verlorenen' unausgesprochen den Vorzug geben, setzen sie das Selbstwertgefühl des zweitgeborenen Überlebenden herab.

3

Schriftsteller sind, so Thomas Mann, raunende Beschwörer des Imperfekts. Denn ihr Metier, das Erzählen, hat viel mit dem Erinnern zu tun. In seinem Romandebüt *Tristanakkord* erfindet Hans-Ulrich Treichel dazu eine ironische Variante: Er läßt seine Hauptfigur, den Germanistikstudenten Georg Zimmer, eine Doktorarbeit beginnen mit dem Thema 'Das Vergessen in der

Literatur'. »Lethe [...] und nicht Mnemosyne« (T, 17) – Vergessen, nicht Erinnerung, schwört ihn sein Doktorvater bei der Vorbesprechung auf das Thema ein. Denn übers Erinnern gab es zuhauf Dissertationen, nicht aber übers Vergessen. Nur hier konnte sich der arbeitslose Doktorand und Sozialhilfeempfänger Georg Zimmer akademische Sporen verdienen. Sie benötigte er dringend. Doch da, während er erwartungsvoll nach Zitaten und Texten über das Vergessen sucht, kommt ihm der Zufall zu Hilfe. Ein erkrankter Freund hatte ihn an seiner Statt als Ersatz empfohlen: als Hilfe für den Komponisten Bergmann, der gerade in Schottland auf dem Landsitz eines englischen Komponisten seine Lebenserinnerungen überarbeitete. Bergmann, erfährt Zimmer, ist nicht irgendwer, sondern der »bedeutendste [...] lebende deutsche Komponist«, »eine Art Brahms oder Beethoven« (T, 21).

Die Bibliothekarin des Musikwissenschaftlichen Instituts teilt ihm mit, daß über keinen lebenden deutschen Komponisten so viel publiziert wurde und werde wie über Bergmann; in den einschlägigen Nachschlagewerken wie *Musik in Geschichte und Gegenwart* findet er mehrseitige Werkverzeichnisse. Treichel etabliert in der Figurenkonstellation einen farbig-witzigen Gegensatz: Hier das 'Genie', dort die Hilfskraft. Denn in der Musik hat es Georg Zimmer nicht weit gebracht. Als humoreske Schnurre erzählt Treichel wie auf den quälenden Blockflötenunterricht in der Grundschule nach der obligaten Begeisterung für die Beatles der verzweifelte Versuch gefolgt war, der Gitarre mächtig zu werden. Doch das scheiterte ebenso wie die Anstrengung, das Klavierspiel zu erlernen. Bereits Beethovens leichteres Klavierstück 'Für Elise' zeigte die Grenzen seines Talents auf. Zu mehr als »einem mechanischen Herumdrücken« (T, 32), läßt Treichel spöttisch seines Helden Klavierlehrer befinden, war er nicht in der Lage. Verlangt aber hat der Komponist Bergmann nicht nach seinen musikalischen Fertigkeiten, sondern nach seiner Fähigkeit, mit Sprache und Manuskripten umzugehen. Eine abwechslungsreich geschilderte Anreise führt Georg Zimmer mit Flugzeug und Airshuttle bis auf die Innere Hebrideninsel Skye. Schließlich auf der autofreien Äußeren Hebrideninsel Scarp angekommen, sollte ihn Bergmann selbst abholen:

Als Georg sich [...] umdrehte, sah er jemanden den Weg herunterkommen. Das mußte Bergmann sein [...]. Bergmann ging sehr langsam den Weg Richtung Anlegestelle hinunter. Gelegentlich blieb er sogar stehen und ruderte mit den Armen. Dann ging er weiter, noch immer die Arme in der Luft schwingend, um wieder abrupt stehenzubleiben. Nun aber wie erstarrt, ohne die geringste Armbewegung und mit nach unten gesenktem Kopf. Wenn Bergmann so weitermacht, dachte Georg, würde es Nacht werden, bis der Komponist bei ihm angekommen war. (*T*, 35–6)

Anlässe zur Irritation gibt es in *Tristanakkord* für den Doktoranden Georg Zimmer etliche. Mit Sinn für Komik hat Treichel in Bergmann die Figur eines Künstlers porträtiert, der alles seiner Produktivität sowie der Pflege seines Ruhms unterordnet. Nicht nur bei Spaziergängen, sondern auch in Gegenwart anderer Menschen rudert Bergmann mit den Armen, läßt sie schwingen und stößt dabei rhythmische Zischlaute aus, das heißt er dirigiert und komponiert. Er macht sich alles zunutze: Zeit, Räume, Menschen. Bereits die Skizzen der gerade entstehenden Kompositionen reicht er an seinen Sekretär weiter – der zugleich über ihn promoviert und der jede neue Partiturseite analysiert und interpretiert. Und Mary, Tochter eines seiner Uraufführungsdirigenten, hilft ihm bei der Reinschrift. »Rein mengenmäßig« kann Bergmann bei derartigem Arbeitstempo »mit seinen großen Kollegen mithalten« (*T*, 21) – mit Bach, Mozart und Wagner.

Treichel ist ein gewitzter Erzähler. In seinem Satzbau bevorzugt er Wiederholung und Variation. Scheinbare Pedanterie und Detailtreue erwecken den Eindruck der Verzögerung, fast des Stillstandes. Bergmann gewinnt so an Statur und Prägnanz: Als zum Egoismus berechtigtes Genie, als Mann äußerster Effizienz. Und der wie Treichel alle Register der Häme, des Spotts, der Bosheit und der Pikiertheit zu ziehen versteht, wenn etwas seinen Vorstellungen nicht entspricht oder wenn sein Rivale Nerlinger ins Spiel kommt. Mit lapidaren Dialogen und in kurzweiligen Beschreibungen parodiert Treichel genüßlich den Musikbetrieb, den Interpretationsjargon und das vermeintliche Kennertum sowie die Nöte eines Doktoranden der Germanistik – meisterliche Etüden. Zu erkennen ist hinter Treichels Figur Bergmann in Umrissen der Komponist Hans Werner Henze, für den Treichel selbst als Librettist gearbeitet hat.

Tristanakkord ist ein gelungener Romanakkord, in dem Treichel die Welt der Kunst und der Wissenschaft, der Musik, Literatur und der Germanistik zu einem zwischen Ironie und Skurillität, Lebensernst und Kunstspiel changierendem Wohlklang zusammenfügt.

4

Italiensehnsucht und Italienliebe führt den Berliner Kunstgeschichtsstudenten Albert in Hans-Ulrich Treichels zweitem Roman *Der irdische Amor* nach Rom. Doch die Stadt, in der er sich einen Lebenstraum erfüllen will, weist ihn ab: Als ein in seinem Hotelzimmer zufällig mitnächtigender deutscher Drogendealer verhaftet wird, 'rät' die Polizei dem Studenten Albert, Italien so schnell wie möglich zu verlassen. Wieder in Berlin, in der Enge seines Schöneberger Dachzimmers, treibt ihn seine plötzlich wieder aufflammende Italiensehnsucht ins 'Montestella', in ein italienisches Lokal, das ihm schon vor seiner mißglückten Romreise aufgefallen war. Als sich in der leeren Bar nichts regt, will Albert wieder gehen. Doch da erscheint eine junge Frau:

> Die Frau hatte dunkles, fast blauschwarzes Haar und ebenso dunkle Augen. Sie war schlank, aber nicht knabenhaft, sondern sehr weiblich, was wohl auch daran lag, daß sie ein schwarzes und ziemlich enges Cocktailkleid trug. Außerdem hatte sie das Tablett auf der flachen Hand getragen und hierbei einen solchen Hüftschwung vollführt, wie Albert ihn bisher nur aus Filmen kannte, die auf Sizilien spielten und in denen dunkle Schönheiten über mittaghelle Plätze gingen. (*iA*, 41)

Es ist Elena, in die sich der Student Albert im 'Montestella', einem als Bar getarnten illegalen Spielclub, verliebt. Oder besser gesagt: es ist das Bild, das er sich von der Frau macht, die er in Elena zu lieben glaubt: eine Klischeemischung aus Autogrammbildern von Claudia Cardinale, Sophia Loren und Jayne Mansfield. Es ist dieser Unterschied zwischen Vorstellung und Wirklichkeit, zwischen Sehnsucht und Realität, mit dem Hans-Ulrich Treichel in *Der irdische Amor* auf ebenso originelle wie kurzweilige Art das Thema der Liebe und Sexualität umspielt. Treichel, im Distanzherstellen geübter Poetikdozent, faltet sein Sujet in etlichen Analogien auseinander. Mit glücklicher Finderhand hat er sie dem dafür üppigen Motivschatz der Kunstgeschichte entnommen – zum Beispiel in Gestalt von Caravaggios Gemälde 'Amore vincitore', 'Der siegreiche Amor'. Es hängt in seinem Roman noch in der alten Dahlemer Gemäldegalerie (heute im neuen Museum im Tiergarten) und zeigt einen auf einem Faltenwurf ruhenden nackten Jüngling. Er ist Gegenstand des Referats, das Treichels Student Albert im Examenskolloquium von Professor Delbrück, dem Leiter des Kunsthistorischen Instituts der Freien Universität, gehalten hat. Allerdings nicht zur Zufriedenheit seines Professors. Denn während Caravaggios 'Amore vincitore' den bevorstehenden Eroberungen unbefangen-siegessicher und »beneidenswert unbe-kümmert und selbstsicher« (*iA*, 27) entgegensieht, interpretiert Albert den Faltenwurf, auf dem der Jüngling ruht, als weibliche Scham. Professor Delbrück, eine »Koryphäe der Caravaggioforschung« (*iA*, 25), weist dies als sexistische Deutung mit der Bemerkung zurück, daß Albert »Kunstgeschichte mit Gynäkologie« (*iA*, 31) verwechsle und daß es ihm – wohl weil ihm eine Freundin fehle – an Distanz zu seinem Gegenstand mangele. Treichel, wieder sich mit den Mitteln der Ironie und der Umkehrung Spielraum verschaffend, versteht es glänzend, diesen Mangel darzustellen. Denn während Caravaggios Amor vom »erwachenden Geschlechtstrieb« »beflügelt« (*iA*, 27) scheint, war und ist es bei Treichels Liebesgott Albert anders, weil höchst irdisch: Er ist kein strahlender Eroberer, sondern ein Verlierer, der sich immer schon von seiner Sexualität »zernagt und angefressen« (*iA*, 27) fühlt. Nicht erst mit der Pubertät, sondern bereits seit dem Säuglingsalter leidet er unter seinem »ständig juckenden Pubertätskörper« (*iA*, 27), unter Verspannungen und »verschleppter Dauererregung« (*iA*, 18). Vor allem aber unter fehlendem Selbstbewußtsein und ständiger Befangenheit. Albert wurde ein schwieriger und renitenter Schüler, der sich nach der Lektüre von Bronislaw Malinowskis ethnologischer Studie *Geschlechtstrieb und Verdrängung bei den Primitiven* hineinträumte in das ungehemmte, paradiesisch anmutende Sexualleben der Trobriand-Melanesier. Aber weder diese Idealisierung noch Wilhelm Reichs Bücher *Die Funktion des Orgasmus* und *Die sexuelle Revolution* helfen ihm: Statt sich in ihnen Aufklärung zu holen, erwirbt er nur weitere Verwirrung und Selbstunsicherheit. Albert versteht, daß auf ihn die Lebensweisheit zutrifft: »Wenn du bedürftig bist, sinken deine Chancen« (*iA*, 109). Und um so den »orkanartigen« (*iA*, 110) Sehnsuchtsstürmen nicht immer hilflos ausgeliefert zu sein, setzte er, sobald ihn ein Mädchen interessierte, ein gleichgültiges Gesicht auf:

> Immer wenn er ein gleichgültiges Gesicht machte, wurde dies als Zeichen seiner Gleichgültigkeit verstanden. Auf diese Weise konnten

Der Erzähler Hans-Ulrich Treichel

Wochen, Monate, ja sogar Jahre vergehen, und nichts geschah. Einen Großteil seiner Jugend hatte er damit zugebracht, innerlich vor Begehrlichkeit zu glühen und nach außen hin ein gleichgültiges Gesicht zu machen. Mit dem Ergebnis, daß die Zeit verstrich, ohne daß ihm auch nur die geringste Befriedigung zuteil wurde. Wenn er aber kein gleichgültiges Gesicht gemacht hatte, sondern seinen Wünschen gefolgt war, dann war er meistens enttäuscht worden. Er hatte der Welt mutig ein »Ich will dich!« zugerufen, und die Welt hatte ihm schmallippig mit »Ich dich aber nicht!« geantwortet. (*iA*, 110–11)

Kurzweilig schildert Treichel in einigen Episoden, wie Alberts Annäherungsversuche scheitern – zum Beispiel in der Vorlesung eines amerikanischen Gastprofessors, der über die vielfache Darstellung von Nacktheit und menschlichen Geschlechtsmerkmalen in der christlichen Kunst doziert. Anders geht es Albert bei Elena, der Barkeeperin aus dem 'Montestella'. Doch als die ihm beim Rendezvous im Tiergarten ein »Poveretto« (*iA*, 75) – mein Ärmster – nachruft, treibt ihn seine mißverstehende Selbstunsicherheit erst einmal wieder von ihr weg. Um sich abzulenken, schickt Treichel, mit allen Wassern des feinen Spotts gewaschen, seinen Amor in die vermeintlich abkühlende Arena des Sports. Im Berliner Postsportverein in der Moabiter Sporthalle unweit des Gefängnisses beginnt er – als »Folge von zuviel Hemingwaylektüre (*iA*, 77) – mit dem Boxtraining, muß aber schon beim ersten Sparring erkennen, daß er in dieser »rohen und primitiven Sportart« (*iA*, 79) seine körperlichen Voraussetzungen überschätzt hat. Er wechselt zu Judo. Aber auch dieser sportlich vermeintlich »*Sanfte Weg*« (*iA*, 79) hat mit seinen Halte- und Würgegriffen für Albert unangenehme Seiten. Schließlich dreht er auf der Aschenbahn des Wilmersdorfer Stadions regelmäßig seine Runden, bis ihn ein penibler Platzwart mit seinem »Runter vom Rasen!« (*iA*, 85) peinigt und er Zuflucht im Schwimmbad sucht. Doch auch der Sport kann seine Sehnsucht nach Elena nicht stillen. Als sie in ihre sardische Heimat zurückkehrt, um dort in ihrem Haus ein Kosmetikstudio zu eröffnen, folgt er ihr begeistert. Dort auf Sardinien würde er endlich seine Examensarbeit über Caravaggios 'Ungläubigen Thomas' schreiben – inmitten einer mittelalterlich-toskanischen Renaissancekulisse:

Der Bus war beinahe leer, die Strecke offensichtlich nicht sehr gefragt. Und sehr ansehnlich war sie auch nicht. Albert hatte von Steineichen, Pinienwäldern und roten Porphyrklippen gelesen. Außerdem sollte es

> überall jahrtausendealte Festungstürme geben. Aber das mußte woanders sein. Erst einmal sah Albert nur eine Ausfallstraße, die von Lagerhallen, Tankstellen, einer Raffinerie und verschiedenen Wasserbecken gesäumt wurde, die offenbar der Salzgewinnung dienten. Dann verwandelte sich die Landschaft, wurde hügelig, wenn auch nicht unbedingt schön. Auf jeden Fall waren nun keine Raffinerien mehr zu sehen, sondern Macchia und dazwischen kleinere Wohnsiedlungen, die zumeist aus Neubauten bestanden. Die Fahrt war eintönig und dauerte länger, als Albert erwartet hatte. Irgendwann schlief er ein und erwachte erst wieder, als sie bereits kurz vor Carbonia waren. Das erste, was er sah, waren mit fleckigem Gras bewachsene Halden. Elena hatte ihm gesagt, daß er sich unter Carbonia kein mittelalterliches Städtchen nach Toskanaart vorstellen sollte, sondern eine moderne Bergarbeiterstadt. Sie hatte ihm auch gesagt, daß es mit dem Bergbau inzwischen vorbei sei. Nur mit den Halden war es noch nicht vorbei. Aber das hatte Elena ihm nicht gesagt. (*iA*, 187–8)

Nicht lange bleibt Albert in der aufgegebenen sardischen Bergarbeiterstadt mit ihren Schlackenhalden und dem in faschistischem Stil erbauten Rathaus. Denn bald schon tritt an Elenas Stelle eine deutsche, in ihre Heimat zurückkehrende Studentin – vielmehr das Bild, das er sich von ihr macht. Es war ja auch nicht die Person Elena, die er zu lieben glaubte, sondern die Vorstellung, die er vom Bild der Frau in sich trug. Also scheitert Treichels irdischer Amor ein weiteres Mal.

Treichel hat sein Psychodrama in schönen Analogien und mit psychologischem Feinsinn komödiantisch-heiter erzählt. Der Autor des vergnüglichen Künstlerromans *Tristanakkord* ist auch in seinem neuen Roman *Der irdische Amor* ein *poeta doctus*. Im studentischen und Dozentenmilieu, im wissenschaftlichem Balzgehabe kennt er sich ebenfalls bestens aus. Wie Klaus Modick und Jochen Schimmang gehört Hans-Ulrich Treichel zu den Autoren der mittleren Generation, die mit Sinn für Affekte und Effekte erzählen – ohne literaturtheoretische Verkrampfung und kunstideologische Verspannung.

5

'Schlüsselszenen der Erfahrung':[1] (Dis)location in the Prose Work of Hans-Ulrich Treichel

DAVID BASKER

The lectures which Hans-Ulrich Treichel gave in 2000 as his 'Frankfurter Poetikvorlesungen' and which were published under the title *Der Entwurf des Autors* in the same year, are personal accounts of selected aspects of the author's life broadly connected with his literary career. Treichel's presentation of autobiographical detail is, in turn, repeatedly set against his reading of works of literature and of their authors' lives. At the same time, each of the essays has a very clear geographical frame of reference; indeed, setting (in place and time) is the most obvious structuring principle for the five lectures and place is evidently crucial in Treichel's understanding of how he became a writer. The current chapter will take as its starting point an analysis of how the settings of each of the sections of *Der Entwurf des Autors* are presented. In the light of this analysis, the significance of geographical settings for each of Treichel's works of prose fiction will then be examined.

The five essays in *Der Entwurf des Autors* appear largely in the chronological order of Treichel's own life: childhood, student days, and experiences in adult life connected with his progress as a writer. Underpinning this development through time is a movement through space which is close to, but not identical with, the stages in Treichel's career. According to this geographical scheme, the first essay, 'Lektionen der Leere' focuses on the town in 'Ostwestfalen' where the author grew up, but also addresses some of the questions raised by his family's origins in eastern Europe and in Swabia; the essay covering the period of his studies, 'Berlin – Terra Incognita', is located very obviously in West Berlin, but measures Treichel's perspective on the city against his view of his home province; 'Geographie des Sehnens' describes, in theory and practice, the author's experience of European travel as a young adult; 'Rom oder die Mittagsdämonen' has a rather more specific geographical focus, covering Treichel's time as a 'Stipendiat' at the Villa Massimo, but once again using the setting of his childhood as a yardstick; and in 'Raucherbedarfsartikel', the final essay of the volume, Treichel mixes the continuing narration of his stay in Rome, including the genesis of the volume *Von Leib und Seele*, with more early memories of Versmold.

If we now examine in more detail Treichel's presentation of each of these geographical settings in turn, it is clear that his childhood in northern Germany represents a set of influences to which he repeatedly returns. 'Lektionen der Leere' establishes a set of contrasts between ideal and reality. Under normal circumstances, Treichel contends, childhood is 'das sonnenbeschienene Griechenland auf der Landkarte der eigenen Lebensgeschichte' (*EA*, 11); and a series of childhoods of famous writers – Plutarch, Rousseau, Fontane, Goethe, Ernest Hemingway, J. M. R. Lenz, to name but a few – is adduced as evidence that, happy or unhappy, an interesting childhood can be an important step on the road to literary success. These observations are set against Treichel's view of his own early years: 'Die Leere der Kindheit ist ohne Zweifel meine prägendste Kindheitserfahrung' (*EA*, 16). The cluttered parental home (which doubled as a shop), the featureless landscape of 'Ostwestfalen' and the sheer boredom of life in a small, provincial town led to 'ein heftiges Fernweh': 'Damals wußte ich nur, daß ich raus wollte, weg – wohin war egal' (*EA*, 19).

The powerful sense of emptiness in the present of Treichel's childhood is only exacerbated by the complex feelings he develops towards the family past in East Prussia, as a result of his parents' reaction to their traumatic wartime experiences. They are 'Heimatvertriebene', refugees who only came to Westphalia because they had to. The trauma of the experience of flight at the end of the Second World War – a trauma which, as we shall see, is reworked in a number of ways in Treichel's fiction[2] – means that the family deliberately suppresses its own past: 'Die Eltern, die ich kennengelernt hatte, waren Eltern ohne Vergangenheit. Und daß hieß für mich zuallererst: Eltern ohne Eltern. [. . .] Alles, was gewesen war, schien ausgelöscht und brachte sich erst mit der Zeit und auf Umwegen erneut in Erinnerung' (*EA*, 21). Indeed, we do not learn exactly where the family came from in this essay; the absence of the place name stands for the many details that were suppressed and that together left Treichel without the family context that normally establishes childhood identity. The family's home in eastern Europe is a non-place, since it exists neither in political fact as far as the limits of Germany are now concerned nor in the parents' willingness to engage with their memories. At the end of the essay, Treichel powerfully expresses the result of the combination of a featureless home town and a dislocated family history:

> Der Osten sagte mir ebensowenig wie mir Ostwestfalen sagte, was ja auch eine Art Osten war. Ich sehnte mich nicht nach einer verlorenen Heimat. Ich sehnte mich aber sehr wohl nach der Erfüllung einer Leere, die meine Kindheit war. Und zugleich mußte ich feststellen, daß diese Sehnsucht sich mir als eine Art Heimweh vermittelte. Als Heimweh ohne Heimat. (*EA*, 29).

If Treichel's childhood and family background were sources of disorientation, his move to West Berlin as a student, as described in 'Berlin – Terra Incognita', provided some relief from the emptiness of Westphalia, albeit in a limited and rather curious way. Certainly, West Berlin, as Treichel describes it, is not very pretty to look at, its citizens are justly famous for their rudeness, and his first room in the city is 'keine Heimat [. . .] aber es war – alles in allem – die vorerst beste Heimatlosigkeit, die ich mir vorstellen konnte' (*EA*, 32). It is West Berlin's geopolitical position that offers Treichel relief from the personal burden of his childhood: 'Der Berliner hatte keine Macht über mich, weil Ostwestfalen – mit anderen Worten: meine Kindheit – in Berlin keine Macht über mich hatte.' The price, however, is a high one: 'Dies aber verdankte sich vor allem der Tatsache, daß Westberlin von einer Mauer und einem sich daran anschließenden Korridor, genannt DDR, umgeben war, der mich vor Ostwestfalen und meiner Kindheit schützte. Die Mauer war mein antiwestfälischer Schutzmauer' (*EA*, 32). The borders comfort Treichel and the sense of being an – admittedly passive – witness to historical events is agreeable, even though, as his comic irony indicates, dividing a nation to make a provincial north German feel at home is a somewhat high price to pay. Like Westphalia, West Berlin seems empty, but place matters; for Treichel this is a more comforting 'Leere ohne Tod und mit Perspektive' (*EA*, 37). It is a city that leads the author somewhere, as the extended analogy Treichel makes with the 'Berliner Zimmer' as a 'Durchgangs- und

Schwellenraum' (*EA*, 37) suggests. Despite the drawbacks of the city, the connection between a sense of belonging and literary activity is made explicit in the essay: Berlin allows Treichel to write his first poems.

The third and fourth essays in the collection deal primarily with Treichel's attitude towards, and experience of, southern Europe. 'Geographie des Sehnens' begins by describing his views on Europe in terms of points of the compass. While acknowledging that everything is relative, he notes that he has in common with many northern Europeans a longing to experience the south. Treichel cites numerous literary examples of the phenomenon and is largely nonplussed by the interest of the likes of Andersch or Enzensberger in northern Europe. A combination of the exotic and the cultural associations of southern Europe – 'Nymphen gab es [in Ostwestfalen] nirgends' (*EA*, 65) – draws Treichel spiritually towards the Mediterranean, but, when the theory is put into practice, his experiences are not quite as fulfilling as he had hoped. In Provence as a young adult, for example, he feels alienated: 'Südfrankreich stimmte mich eher schwermütig, denn es kam mir durch und durch französisch vor, und es schien ganz so, als wollte er französisch bleiben. Es erlaubte mir kein Gefühl der Zugehörigkeit, [. . .] und ich fühlte mich zurückgestoßen' (*EA*, 66). He subsequently follows the German fashion for visiting Crete, but is similarly disappointed: 'Ich verstand die Griechen nicht, und die Griechen verstanden mich nicht' (*EA*, 67).

The failure to integrate into southern Europe culturally or linguistically is a deflating experience for Treichel, but he tries again, and 'Rom oder die Mittagsdämonen' describes a stay in Rome which gives him the opportunity to fulfil his yearning for the south. Again, Treichel is able to cite many literary precedents, both among the works of the recipients of an award from the Villa Massimo and in the German literary canon as a whole. Treichel's own experience of Rome is an overwhelmingly lonely one. He sees himself as just one in the series of 'verirrte Schafe' (*EA*, 84) who are the German beneficiaries of the Villa Massimo prize. The city is searingly hot, very unwelcoming and fails to satisfy any of his emotional or professional needs, which are numerous: 'Besonders der in Ostwestfalen geborene Schriftsteller möchte in Italien und speziell in Rom erlöst werden: von seiner Einsamkeit, seiner Geschichtsferne, seiner emotionalen Bemoostheit, seiner Mythen-leere, von seiner inneren Pinien- und Zypressenlosigkeit insgesamt' (*EA*, 86). 'Erlösung' of this sort is not available in modern Rome and the loneliness of Treichel's stay powerfully brings back to him the emptiness of his childhood in Versmold. His personal perception of the city is of a place which is 'nicht frei von westfälischer Ausweglosigkeit' (*EA*, 92).

Paradoxically, the parallel between the disappointing experiences in Rome – loneliness, alienation, writer's block as far as poetry is concerned – and the boredom of growing up in Versmold gives Treichel the impulse to turn to prose writing. It is the fictional reworking of childhood memories that eventually leads to the volume *Von Leib und Seele*, the origins of which are sketched out in 'Raucherbedarfsartikel', the final essay of *Der Entwurf des Autors*. The title refers to the smoking paraphernalia which his father stocked in his shop in Versmold and which momentarily caught the imagination of Treichel as a boy. It is the 'Seelenleere' (*EA*, 104) of modern-day Rome that brings to the surface this sort of echo of the past and feeds Treichel's creative energies:

> Insofern war es die Erfahrung der Langeweile in der Villa Massimo, [. . .] die den autobiographischen Schreibimpuls ausgelöst und damit natürlich auch den leeren Raum überhaupt erst erträglich gemacht hat. Wohl kann ich deshalb meine Genese als Prosaautor in Rom ansiedeln – aber ich kann und muß sie zugleich auch in den Leerräumen der Kindheit verorten, denen ich in Rom auf besondere Weise wiederbegegnet bin. (*EA*, 104).

In the essays of *Der Entwurf des Autors*, then, Treichel explains his development as a writer through an appealing mixture of autobiographical detail and erudite reference to the context of (mainly European) literary forebears. It is striking that each stage in this development has a very clear geographical setting; and these settings are not simply backgrounds, but are part of Treichel's sense of identity and of his engagement with the creative act of writing. Overall, the essays present an image of someone who is at odds with his geographical environment, in the widest sense. Thus, for example, Treichel is aware of his family background, located somewhere in eastern Europe, only as a painful and somehow shameful absence; and his childhood experience of Westphalia is of emptiness, boredom and a need to escape. West Berlin offers relief to some extent and it is here that he is able to write poetry for the first time, but the city is presented as the best of a bad lot and unification threatens to bring 'Ostwestfalen' closer to home once again. As far as the experience of foreign climes is concerned, the essays describe an unsettling and ultimately disappointing discrepancy between expectation – of enjoyment of the exotic and culturally stimulating – and reality: southern Europe is linguistically and culturally disorientating, a lonely, at times unfriendly place for Treichel and it is only the boredom of Rome that triggers his career as a writer of prose fiction. The question remains as to how these key experiences of place, which Treichel chose, after all, to highlight so clearly in the series of 'Poetikvorlesungen', influence his fiction.

As *Der Entwurf des Autors* indicates, Treichel began as a writer of prose fiction with *Von Leib und Seele* (1992), a volume of short prose extracts based heavily on his own biography; a second volume of prose pieces appeared as *Heimatkunde* in 1996. The two collections of short extracts show very clear geographical correspondences with the account of Treichel's career set out in *Der Entwurf des Autors*. *Von Leib und Seele* is written as a series of separate but connected descriptions of stages in an unnamed first-person narrator's life. The narrator's childhood in 'Ostwestfalen', which is addressed in the opening section, reflects closely the author's own experience; the process of 'Umerinnerung' which creative writing involves for Treichel allows him to paint a fuller picture of life in northern Germany in the 1950s than in the volume of essays.[3] Particularly striking are the adjectives which the narrator uses to characterize his experiences: the houses are 'trübsinnig', the people 'äußerst verschlossen' and 'mißgünstig' (*VLS*, 7). There is considerable resentment of the commercial success of the narrator's family, who are 'Heimatvertriebene', among the native population. The story offers deeper insight into the relationship with the past of a family in this situation than the volume of essays does, because the narrator recalls disconnected moments when the family discuss their lost home in the East and their attitudes towards Russians (who are held responsible for all the terrible things that have befallen the family) and Poles (shabby, disorganized people and figures of fun). What emerges most powerfully from this description is the confusion in which the unfulfilled need to belong to a place leaves the young narrator. Born in Westphalia he is nevertheless rejected by the locals as an outsider because of his family; and his family offer only a confusing set of memories of the strange place from which they have come and of which the narrator is unable to conceive a 'genaues Bild' (*VLS*, 10). The Swabian branch of the family only confuses matters further. The psychological effect on the narrator is twofold: he rejects the family past, regarding his parents as 'heimatlos' (*VLS*, 13); and he begins to overeat.

Section IV of *Von Leib und Seele* offers the reader a slightly modified perspective on 'Ostwestfalen' as the now adult narrator returns to his birthplace to celebrate his brother's birthday. It is an awkward return both at the level of family relations and as far as the narrator's sense of where he comes from is concerned. The story interweaves comic irony over the family relationships in the narrative present and poignant observations about the past. The imagery used to describe the narrator's sense of childhood place is funny and sad at the same time: his home town lives inside him 'wie ein jederzeit angriffsbereiter Virus im Leibe' (*VLS*, 39). The conclusion to the episode confirms the discomforting relationship which the narrator has with his childhood. As he looks at a picture of himself with his brother as happy, close children, he realizes that nothing good from that past remains with him:

> Ich konnte mich weder an den Spielplatz noch an auch nur einen einzigen vergnügten Nachmittag in Gesellschaft meines ältesten Bruders erinnern. Falls es ihn wirklich gegeben hat, dann war er wie alles Erfreuliche, was mir in meiner Kindheit möglicherweise widerfahren ist, unwiderbringlich verschollen. (*VLS*, 45)

Three of the eight sections which comprise *Von Leib und Seele* are played out during the narrator's adult life in West Berlin. Two of these are comic accounts of the bizarre psychotherapeutic treatment which the narrator goes through, and here too there is resentment about the circumstances of his childhood; they are attempts to free himself from the 'Bedrückung meiner Kindheit' (*VLS*, 17). As in *Der Entwurf des Autors*, Berlin thus represents a place where the adult seeks relief from 'Ostwestfalen'. Three more sections of the collection show the narrator travelling abroad from Berlin: to Salerno and to Lublin in search of employment and to Rome to accept a literary prize of dubious value. Foreign places are disconcerting to the narrator, all the more so since the customary stereotypes are deflated. Salerno in deepest winter, for example, has nothing of the gentle climate normally associated with southern Europe and the sea has all the appeal of a dirty 'Betonfläche' (*VLS*, 29). The hotel is empty and unwelcoming, the locals try to exploit the narrator and he feels entirely isolated. Similarly, when he travels to Rome to try and sort out the details of his job his expectations of finding a more open, better organized and friendlier place are dashed; he finds the capital crowded but just as unwelcoming as Salerno. Even at a personal level in Rome, he is treated with little hospitality by his boss's husband and she fails to appear at all to sort out his problems. Buying all of the German-language newspapers he can find is clearly a desperate attempt to overcome the disorientation of being abroad for the narrator. The second description in the volume of a trip to Rome expresses a similar constellation of feelings: the literary prize for which he has been nominated is clearly of little value, in terms of either prestige or financial reward. As in other descriptions of foreign travel, the linguistic barrier leaves Treichel's narrator confused, disconsolate and alone. Nor does he feel any more at home in his experience of northern Europe. The narrator's meeting with the fellow Germanist who is ready to employ him in Lublin leads only to an argument about academic publications which is based on a mutual lack of cultural understanding. The terms of the narrator's employment are confusing and impractical and the sudden loneliness he feels when he sees the accommodation that has been prepared for him is typical of the experience of foreign places in much of Treichel's writing. It is also typical that the negative attitude is revealed to be subjective; once the narrator has decided not to stay in Poland, the burden that has been lifted changes his perspective: 'Und zum ersten Mal fühlte ich eine Anhänglichkeit an die polnische Landschaft und die Menschen, die ich hier getroffen hatte' (*VLS*, 55). In the same way, the narrator's observation at the beginning of the extract as he arrives in Poland recalls many similar episodes of foreign travel in Treichel's work: 'Und hier, in diesem südpolnischen Bahnhofsbüffet [. . .] überfiel mich, wie so oft, wenn ich auf Reisen war, das Gefühl, ein wurzellos umherirrender, völlig vereinsamter Mensch zu sein' (*VLS*, 47).

Heimatkunde oder Alles ist heiter und edel, Treichel's second volume of prose extracts, consists of a series of portraits from the first-person narrator's life which are structured in terms of setting around now familiar coordinates: childhood in northern Germany, student life in Berlin, and the experience of a variety of 'foreign' places, some of which are simply unfamiliar towns in Germany. The first five of the 'Besichtigungen' in the volume cover the narrator's early years in 'Ostwestfalen', including the details of his birth, the idiosyncracies of his father and of the 'Helden des Rauchens' who buy tobacco from him. The extract entitled 'Der Negerpastor' confirms the hierarchies which obtained in eastern Europe and which are hinted at elsewhere in Treichel's versions of his family past: although the narrator's father speaks Russian and Polish, he does not consider these capabilities to be 'Bildungsgüter' (*H*, 40), since he looks down on the Slavonic cultures of his home; the eponymous cleric, however, is a true scholar in the father's eyes because he can speak Latin. The subsequent section, which gives the title to the volume, offers a very discomforting view of schooldays in northern Germany. The teacher of 'Heimatkunde' is proud of everything that 'Ostwestfalen' has to offer and tries, during the predictable school field trips, to awaken a similar 'Heimatstolz' in his charges (*H*, 47). The narrator, by contrast, sees nothing to distinguish his home town, its environs or its flora and fauna. The locals are as 'versteinert' as the 'Externsteine' that he is forced to visit with the school (*H*, 52) and the list of adjectives that describe the place and its people are damning: 'düster', 'naßkalt', 'traurig', 'verregnet', to cite just a few (*H*, 56-7). The narrator fears that he, too, is becoming a petrified Westphalian and concludes: 'Ich saß in der westfälischen Falle' (*H*, 55). The extract also takes the biography one stage further, to the boarding school to which the narrator was sent in Hessen;[4] for the narrator, simply being referred to as a 'Westfale' by the schoolteachers, and thus reminded of the burden of his background, is enough to incur his hatred of everything to do with Hessen.

The West Berlin sections of *Heimatkunde* present almost picaresque accounts of the narrator's experiences: the descriptions of unusual student jobs (in a theatre, for example, and in one of the underground warehouses intended to supply the city in the case of a future Soviet blockade) and of a visit to a Holocaust exhibition in Wannsee show that, for all that the narrator's life in Berlin is strange, its strangeness is an interesting relief to the boredom of childhood. The last four sections of the volume see the narrator travelling away from the city, however, to experience unknown places; and, once again, that experience is seen to be disorientating, at times depressingly so. This is true even of visits to places elsewhere in Germany. In 'Alles ist heiter und edel', in particular, the narrator and his wife have a thoroughly unpleasant visit to the town of Stendal in the former GDR. The train is overcrowded, the journey is uncomfortable and the scenery depressing in its shabbiness. The town of Stendal itself is run-down and still has the characteristic East German stink of burning lignite. Even where western commercialism has tried to renovate – in the form of a Viennese coffee house, for example – the resultant mix of cultures is discordant. The couple are only too relieved to get back to the train, 'wo wir uns mit Kaffee, Aspirin und Rinderkraftbrühe von den Wirren der Zeiten erholten' (H, 110). 'Poetisches Portugal' and 'Auf der Suche nach Venedig' both see the narrator travel to more exotic places than the former GDR, but with equally dismal results. In Portugal, above all, the barrier of language is thematized. The narrator and the 'Sekretär' who looks after him communicate on the common but shaky ground of weak English and the narrator is unable to follow the disagreement which he witnesses in a restaurant. His ostensible reason for being in Portugal is subject to linguistic confusion too; it is not clear whether he is there to translate a Portuguese poet's work into German, or to have his own poetry translated. In the bizarre setting of a dilapidated castle, the narrator, who is only there in any case as a substitute for someone more famous, manages a translation of a Camões poem by virtue of a linguistic invention which he hopes no one will notice; when a Portuguese translator of German arrives, however, the game is up and the narrator is forced to leave the castle in humiliation. The description gives rise to some moments of comic irony, not least through the faulty translation, but in the end the section describes the failure of intercultural communication and the embarrassing discomfort that results from it. 'Auf der Suche nach Venedig' illustrates once again the discrepancy between attractive stereotypes and disappointing reality. The narrator and his wife are simply unable to follow in Goethe's footsteps in approaching Venice, since no tourist route exists along the Brenta, and: 'Je näher wir Venedig kommen, desto düsterer wird das Bild' (H, 126). Modern Venice shatters any romantic illusions the narrator might have; the gondolas are shabby, the hotel is noisy and the streets seem dangerous at night. Once again, the experience of a foreign place ends on a very discordant note: 'Wir gehen zurück zur Pension und fallen, von

Hupen, Hörnern und Sirenen begleitet, in den traumschweren venezianischen Schlaf' (*H*, 131).

The short descriptive passages of *Von Leib und Seele* and *Heimatkunde* are evidently based closely on episodes from Treichel's own life and offer clear evidence that the notion of being out of step with one's geographical place is an important creative impulse in his work. The theme of Treichel's first longer piece of prose, *Der Verlorene*, has its origin in the psychological trauma of family loss and, on one level, exists independently of place.[5] At the same time, the geographical settings of the work map out the trauma and its effects and reveal a narrator who is just as far out of step with his surroundings as his counterparts in Treichel's shorter prose. The key geographical opposition in the novel is between the life of the first-person narrator as a child in 'Ostwestfalen' and his family's background in East Prussia. These details are obviously based on Treichel's biography, although the process of 'Umerinerrung' brings certain adjustments;[6] above all, what distinguishes *Der Verlorene* from other reworkings of his family biography is the very powerful sense that the two places are separated by traumatic experience.

The family's life in the east of the German *Reich* is, of course, only known to the narrator at second hand, through the remarks of his parents and the other *Heimatvertriebene* whom they know. The fact that this information is difficult to get hold of for the narrator points towards the key tension in *Der Verlorene*; his mother frequently represses the horror of the loss of her child and the sexual assault at the hands of Russian soldiers and simply refuses to speak about the past. Although he is not sure exactly what life in the east was like, the narrator feels that it must have been bad and he cannot understand why the photograph of his missing brother shows him smiling, 'schließlich war Krieg, außerdem befand er sich im Osten, und trotzdem freute er sich' (*V*, 7). Similarly, before he knows the details of his brother's loss, the narrator ascribes his parents' inability to enjoy their leisure time to the tradition of joyless hard work which comes from 'ihrer einerseits schwäbischpietistischen und andererseits ostpreußischen Herkunft' (*V*, 19). It is clear that the father's morality, modesty and Protestant work ethic – this is the third time that he has successfully rebuilt his life – have their origins in the east, as is indicated by the repeated references to what it is fitting for 'ein Bauer aus Rakowiec' to do.[7]

These values mean little to the adolescent, increasingly uncooperative narrator.

The family past, then, is literally and figuratively a foreign country for the narrator. The present is a version of life in 'Ostwestfalen' which is not just marked by emptiness, but by feelings of shame and guilt which, to begin with at least, have no clear roots. The early sections of the text – before it is revealed to the narrator that his parents believe that they may have found the missing Arnold – echo the excerpts describing childhood in the collections of Treichel's shorter prose. Here, too, childhood is a lonely and joyless experience, and the narrator is happiest not when he is being marched around the local countryside by his parents on their Sunday afternoon excursions, but when he manages to persuade them to leave him at home on his own. The slices of Westphalian life in the 1950s that we see are very clearly marked in the text by a pervading sense of unhappiness for all the family; this manifests itself in the narrator's overeating and awkwardness, in his mother's silence, and in his father's almost manic devotion to work.[8]

Location also plays a part in *Der Verlorene* as the process of ascertaining the identity of 'Findelkind 2307' develops and the family is required to travel to pursue the investigation. Travel itself is connected with the family trauma and it is clear that the parents would not leave home at all, given the choice: 'alles Reisen schien sie an die Flucht zu erinnern' (*V*, 122). Indeed, the three-day trip to Heidelberg to undergo crude genetic tests is the first and only time that the family goes away together. The narrator suffers from what is probably a psychosomatic form of travel sickness, since the potential consequences of the trip – the return of Arnold – threaten to undermine his position in the family. The Heidelberg which we and the family see is largely the inside of the consulting rooms of the professor (himself a refugee from Rakowiecz) who is charged with determining the genetic connections. When the family does pay a brief visit to the sights of Heidelberg, it is clear that the personal burdens under which they are living entirely overshadow their perception of place. The narrator, for example, uses his recent experience of physical examination to analyse the features of the statues of the 'Flußgötter' (*V*, 119–20). The visit to Heidelberg castle is entirely overshadowed by the dynamics of an increasingly dysfunctional family, and the narrator's resentment is palpable:

'Wenn die Mutter traurig war, dann war sie wegen Arnold traurig. Wenn der Vater nach Heidelberg fuhr, dann fuhr er wegen Arnold nach Heidelberg. Und wenn wir jetzt das Schloß besuchten, dann taten wir auch dies nur wegen Arnold' (V, 121).

In *Der Verlorene*, then, descriptions of place are both closely involved with the immediate cause of the family's problems – loss of *Heimat*, the horrific details of their flight from the east – and reflections of the burden under which the characters are living as a result. The descriptions of the repression of life in 'Ostwestfalen' and of the joyless visit to Heidelberg are more than a retrospective view of life in the *Wirtschaftswunder* years of the Federal Republic; they are reflections of a set of specifically German family problems.

The protagonist of *Tristanakkord*, Treichel's second major prose work, shares with the narrator of *Der Verlorene* a strong sense of dislocation no matter where he goes; he is constantly at odds with himself, with those he encounters and with his surroundings. Such dislocation is the source of embarrassment for the protagonist and of much of the humour in the novel. Georg Zimmer's collaboration with the internationally renowned composer Bergmann gives him the opportunity to travel the world and the novel is organized around three meetings between Georg and Bergmann with clear geographical settings. First, Georg travels via Lewis to the remote Hebridean island of Scarp to help Bergmann put the finishing touches to his memoirs; then, since that work remains unfinished, Georg must follow the composer to Manhattan; and finally he is charged with travelling to Bergmann's luxurious villa in Sicily to write a poem for the choral section of the composer's latest work. These travels round the world in the narrative present are set against the background of fixed coordinates from Georg's life: his childhood in north Germany and his time as a student in Berlin.

That Georg feels a certain amount of disorientation in the first section of the novel, set on Scarp, is not, perhaps, surprising. The Scottish islands are very remote and Georg is clearly a fish out of water: 'eine Reise wie diese hatte er noch niemals gemacht. Bisher war er nur gereist, um Ferien zu machen. Diesmal reiste er, um zu arbeiten' (T, 19). He must take a circuitous, at times hazardous, ferry route to get to Bergmann at all and he must battle against dramatically changeable weather, which is out of step with the heatwave sweeping the rest of Europe. He has no address for his host, there is no telephone box at the quayside on the island of Lewis and when Bergmann's chauffeur Bruno arrives to meet the ferry in Lewis for the first time it is not to look after Georg but to collect a delivery of wine. The remoteness of the geographical setting matches the uncertainty about the arrangements for Georg's arrival, to leave the character extremely disorientated from the very start of his encounters with Bergmann. Only when a rainbow forms and the chauffeur returns to collect Georg is there a moment of hope in an otherwise comically alienating setting. Georg's unsettling experience of the geographical setting mirrors precisely the disorientating relationship he then forms with the eccentric Bergmann and his sinister servant Bruno. Even at his most settled, when Georg is able to enjoy the 'grandioses Wolkentheater' (*T*, 63) on Scarp, he is unable to turn his experiences into poetry: 'Er wollte sein erstes Schottlandgedicht schreiben, es sollte der Anfang eines Zyklus sein, doch nicht der kleinste Schottlandvers wollte ihm gelingen' (*T*, 63).

In contrast to the sheer remoteness of the Scottish isles, Georg's second journey to meet Bergmann is to New York, one of the most visited cities in the world. Indeed, New York's reputation precedes it in Georg's mind: it has become such a fashionable place to visit, even among the unemployed of Kreuzberg, that he reacts against the trend until the Bergmann opportunity presents itself; and even then it is important to Georg's perception of himself that he is once again a business traveller and not a tourist. Nevertheless, he prepares by studying a guide book (although his constant desire not to offend other people means that he cannot refuse the advice of the bookseller in Berlin to buy *New York für Frauen*). Familiarity and preparation count for little once Georg arrives in New York, however, since his experiences there are every bit as disorientating as those on Scarp. A little knowledge can be an unsettling thing, for Georg knows just enough about America to misread any number of situations. His innocence and ignorance of the way things are done in New York, qualities which are evident even on the plane as he identifies each bridge he flies over as the Brooklyn Bridge, come to the fore as he takes a taxi from the airport into the city. The experience is 'seltsam unwirklich' (*T*, 101) and, as Georg enters the city, his sense of unease grows: 'New York, das war bis jetzt eine nur spärlich beleuchtete und so gut wie unbenutzte Autostraße, auf der er sich zusehends kleiner und verlorener fühlte' (T, 104-5). Once installed in his Washington Square hotel, Georg proceeds to behave just like the tourist he was anxious not to be. But tourism for Georg is not a gentle introduction into something new, an experience mediated by a friendly guide; it is comically disorientating. In the Rockefeller Center, he is trapped in the skyscraper's lift by the guards who refuse him access to their respective floors, until he reaches the top floor and the entrance to the Rainbow Room. His perception of the exoticism of the two women at the restaurant's reception is ironically undercut by their laconic dismissal of Georg; Treichel's images deflate Georg's experiences, as they show that those experiences cannot live up to classical models: 'Was hatten die beiden [Empfangsdamen] eigentlich bewacht, fragte er sich, das Paradies oder die Hölle? Er jedenfalls durfte ihr Reich nicht betreten, das Paradies war ihm verschlossen, die Hölle ebenso, [. . .] nun aber fühlte er sich gekränkt und schlecht behandelt' (T, 116).[9] The experience is so disturbing for Georg that he joins the queue for a tour of the NBC studios almost by accident: 'hier war er willkommen, das merkte er sofort' (T, 117); but this, too, is an experience that only makes Georg feel more like an outsider. He cannot join in the quiz which the guide runs because his knowledge of American TV culture is not extensive enough; and, not for the first time in Georg's travels, there is a linguistic barrier that only emphasizes the fact that he does not belong. His English is not good enough for spontaneous communication but, when he takes the time to prepare, his utterances so obviously lack spontaneity that they hit the wrong note. He is even subject to a public display of his fellow tourists' disapproval when his English makes him seem less than enthusiastic about New York: 'plötzlich begannen zuerst Beverly und dann auch einige der anderen Besucher mit den Füßen zu scharren und dazu zu pfeifen. [. . .] Sie pfiffen ihn aus' (T, 121). In Central Park we see a similar sequence of experiences: he does not encounter the types of people whom his guidebook leads him to expect to find in the park; he cannot make himself understood in the lakeside restaurant, with the result that he orders more wine than he can comfortably drink; and his racial prejudices are undermined when the large African-American on whose foot he steps does not pull a knife on him to threaten his life. After a typically idiosyncratic meeting with Bergmann – itself a source of disorientation for Georg – he finds himself back at his hotel in

Washington Square, where even the squirrels of New York seem to break the mould: 'Nur Nüsse mochten [die Squirrels] nicht. Georg hatte ein Squirrel dabei beobachtet, wie es einige hingeworfene Haselnüsse unberührt ließ, statt dessen aber auf die anmutigste Weise ein Ketchupdöschen zwischen die Vorderpfoten nahm und ausleckte' (*T*, 145). Insulted by Bergmann, confused by his experience of New York, Georg is only too happy to return to the familiarity of Berlin and forget about his trip.

The final and shortest section of the novel is played out in Bergmann's villa on the island of Sicily. Sufficiently flattered by the invitation to compose a verse for Bergmann's latest work, Georg travels via Palermo to Bergmann's home in San Vito Lo Capo. There are similarities with the Scottish island setting, which the narrator makes explicit: 'Nur daß das Gras hier nicht grün, sondern schmutziggrau und verbrannt war' (*T*, 202). The villa itself is anything but dirty grey, however, with its swimming pool, opulent rooms and beautiful gardens. In his own personal suite, it seems as if Georg at last might feel comfortable with his surroundings and his chance to make a name for himself: 'Er befand sich im Süden in einem Garten, der beinahe ein Paradiesgarten war, und er war Gast und, wenn alles gutging, auch Mitarbeiter des berühmten Komponisten' (*T*, 212). Yet Georg's confidence is easily shaken by his reading of Hölderlin's 'Mnemosyne':[10] 'Und plötzlich hatte er das Gefühl, daß die sizilianische Dunkelheit sich zu bewegen schien, daß die Schwärze wanderte, vorbeizog an ihm und an seiner Terrasse, und daß sie dabei immer ein wenig dünkler und düsterer wurde' (*T*, 213). Indeed, in this final section Georg's response to his surroundings is most obviously a reflection of his own, vacillating confidence, so that once Bergmann has rejected his poem, he feels alienated once again: 'Er war in Sizilien, in der Villa des berühmten Komponisten, doch wahrscheinlich hatter er gar kein Recht, hier zu sein' (*T*, 232).

The travels which Georg undertakes are punctuated by brief returns to Berlin, where he is making only hesitant progress in his research for a Ph.D. in German literature. Memories of his life in the capital also rise to the surface while he is abroad and it is clear that Berlin, though familiar, is also a setting in which Georg is not always comfortable. Study has brought him no financial security, so that he is dependent on the generosity of the 'Sozialamt' in Kreuzberg for his survival. Work on his doctorate has advanced painstakingly at best and Treichel parodies the theory-ridden abstractions of academic research, which leave Georg feeling confused and inadequate. By contrast, his fellow students seem to know exactly what they are doing. Before his trip to New York, for example, he is made to feel anything but a sophisticated world traveller by the red-headed student who knows her way round Brooklyn, but tells Georg that he is not ready for anything more challenging than the familiar tourist attractions of Manhattan. Similarly, he meets by chance a university acquaintance in New York who is writing a book on the hidden architectural gems of the city; Georg, we then see, cannot even negotiate the Rockefeller Center, never mind tackle the 'Geheimtips' of his friend.

Concerns about his doctorate do not weigh as heavily on Georg, however, as does his north German background. No matter where he goes, he cannot shake off his experiences as a child in Emsland, which seem to have shaped his personality immutably. Echoes of Treichel's description of his own childhood elsewhere are strong: 'Er hatte das Wiesen- und Weideland, das sich um seinen Heimatort ausbreitete und durch das er als Junge endlose, verzweifelte Fahrradfahrten gemacht hatte, immer "Die grüne Hölle" genannt' (T, 13). Thus, throughout the novel, Georg's feelings of inadequacy are given a geographical origin: he is from Emsland and therefore out of place in the big wide world. Time and again he feels that his 'kleinliche, emsländische Natur' (T, 126) rises to the surface at moments when he wants to be a sophisticated man of the world. Most clearly, Georg attributes his painfully embarrassing failure to act on his feelings for the American student Mary to the place in which he grew up: 'er haderte mit sich und seine Befangenheit. Da war es wieder, was er bei sich das Emsfelde-Syndrom nannte' (T, 234).

At the same time, the novel offers an ironic counterpoint to Georg's conviction that a northern German background is an obstacle to feeling at ease with oneself and the world. Bergmann, too, is from Emsland, yet the two men could hardly be more different. Bergmann is full of confidence, widely travelled, fluent in several languages, and at home wherever he is in the world; he has even shaken off the pallid physical appearance which is characteristic of natives of Emsland and, therefore, of Georg. Throughout, the relationship between Bergmann and Georg is marked by a tension between distance and familiarity. Just when Georg begins to feel at ease in the company of the famous composer, he realizes that Bergmann is making fun of him or has simply forgotten who he is. Preoccupation with creative work is the charitable explanation for this carelessness on Bergmann's part; sheer arrogance is perhaps the more likely reason. Either way, the relationship only serves to make Georg feel less at ease. What is more, other, incidental characters throw the disparity in the relationship into further relief. Bruno, in particular, treats Bergmann at times with scarcely concealed disdain; and he has all of the exotic, worldly experience that Georg wishes he had, as the photograph that Georg finds of Bruno with Aristotle Onassis illustrates.

The techniques of portraying a character almost entirely out of step with his environment is one to which Treichel returned in his most recent novel, *Der irdische Amor*. As is the case with Georg's story, much of the humour in *Der irdische Amor* derives from the fact that the protagonist, Albert, is uncomfortable, embarrassed and incompetent in the settings in which he finds himself. Also like Georg, Albert is engaged in academic work in Berlin, but this time Treichel's protagonist is a student of art history; and we see Albert in Italy and Albert at school in Germany, too. The very first line of the novel indicates that he is not where he wants to be: 'Albert war nur widerwillig nach Berlin und in seine Schöneberger Wohnung zurückgekehrt' (*iA*, 7). His reluctance is then explained at some length, by means of one of several flashbacks in the novel: Albert has just returned from a trip to Italy which was intended to help him with his studies. A period learning the language in Perugia, the narrator tells us, goes well for Albert and his two friends. The move to Rome, however, where Albert hoped to research Caravaggio, ends in comic disaster. Suspected of being involved in the crimes of their drug-dealing roommate, Albert and Stefan spend an uncomfortable night locked in a police van in their pyjamas. Not only that, the beautiful policewoman who spends part of the evening guarding them gets Albert sexually excited in a way that his inadequate clothing cannot conceal. As we have seen elsewhere in Treichel's work, this is a scene in which the expectation of what foreign places have to offer and harsh reality are at odds. Albert's view of Italy has been shaped by Pasolini films and an infatuation with Claudia Cardinale; the policewoman, however, is disgusted by Albert and calls him 'Cretino' (*iA*, 17), a designation that haunts him throughout the novel.

Upon their release, Stefan and Albert are strongly advised to leave Italy at their earliest convenience and they sensibly take the advice to heart. Before he leaves the city, however, Albert plays a psychological trick on himself which is also revealing for the sense of dislocation from which so many of Treichel's characters suffer. Although he has barely spent any time in Rome, Albert's last morning sees him walking round the city saying goodbye to his 'favourite' places. No such relationship exists between the character and the place; he is attempting to convince himself that the city did not remain 'vollkommen fremd' (*iA*, 24) to him, even though we have seen powerful evidence to the contrary. It is the behaviour of someone who wants to belong, but does not.

Despite the humiliation of what has happened in Rome, then, when Albert is back in Berlin he still wants to be in Italy: 'Vor allem mußte er sich von Rom verabschieden, was ihm schwerer fiel, als er gedacht hatte. Berlin kam ihm unsäglich grau und trostlos vor' (*iA*, 37). It is not altogether surprising, therefore, that he is attracted to the 'Montestella' pub, which is frequented exclusively by Italians, and to the beautiful Elena who works there. Treichel's narrator is so close to the protagonist that it is not clear how dependent the alluring description of Elena is on Albert's yearning for Italy, but there is evidence later in the novel that Albert's perception of her changes when he loses interest in Italy. For the time being, however, Albert is smitten by the beautiful stereotype:

> Die Frau hatte dunkles, fast blauschwarzes Haar und ebenso dunkle Augen. [. . .] Außerdem hatte sie das Tablett auf der flachen Hand getragen und hierbei solch einen Hüftschwung vollführt, wie Albert ihn bisher nur aus Filmen kannte, die auf Sizilien spielten und in denen dunkle Schönheiten über mittaghelle Plätze gingen. (*iA*, 41)

The relationship with Elena develops more quickly than Albert could have hoped, although this is not without its humiliation. The first sexual encounter between the two characters is comic, not least because of the setting: Elena makes all the running as they are sitting together on a bench in the Berlin zoo. When Albert loses concentration and with it his erection, it seems to him as if the animals are repeating the insult of the Italian policewoman. In fact, it is the sudden memory of Albert's earliest sexual encounters that has disturbed his interest in Elena; the whole of Chapter Three of the novel is devoted to a flashback to the circumstances of his relationship with Katharina, his girlfriend during his time at the boarding school in Hessen where he spent his adolescent years. Through this flashback we learn a set of familiar details about Albert's family background: his parents are refugees from East Prussia who managed to rebuild their lives, to the point where they were able to pay for their son's education. Sex in the open air is the connection between Katharina in the past and Elena in the present, for indoor fraternization between male and female pupils was severely restricted in the school. Things went wrong between Albert and Katharina once he had been caught in her room, however, and the problems in their relationship have a geographical dimension, too. First, the insults which they trade once they begin to argue show a set of regional prejudices: Katharina is 'ein dekadentes süddeutsches Möbelfabrikantenkind', while she calls him 'einen prüden norddeutschen Puritaner' (iA, 64). Second, in an attempt to solve the problems between them, Albert travels to Würzburg to meet Katharina's parents. A journey ends, once again in Treichel's world, in comic humiliation. Albert is intimidated by the opulence of the family villa (recalling, perhaps, Georg's arrival in Bergmann's Manhattan hotel suite or his home in Sicily) and manages consistently to do the wrong thing: he smokes, to the obvious disapproval of Katharina's mother, and wants to cling to his moth-eaten bearskin coat, even though he is hot, as a security blanket 'auf fremdem Territorium' (iA, 67). The contrast with the neat, traditional southern German 'Trachtenkostüm' of the mother could not be greater and the experience makes the reader squirm with embarrassment for Albert. It is the memory of this embarrassment that interferes with the episode in Berlin with Elena.

Despite the sexual failure with which their meeting ends in the zoo, the relationship between Albert and Elena does develop. For a while it seems that she can offer the best of both worlds: she connects Albert with Italy and he is able to induct her into the complexities of German bureaucracy. In this sense, Albert and Elena are opposites in their attitudes to living abroad: Albert was only too keen to go native in Rome, while Elena wants to remain in an Italian cocoon in Berlin and would happily leave all of her official correspondence unopened if Albert did not intervene. The fact that he is able to experience something of southern Europe through the relationship is undoubtedly an important factor in its appeal. Partly as a result of the particular character of the relationship, the mixture of cultures which we witness in Berlin is striking. The city which the couple inhabit is a strange mixture of the traditional and the bizarrely exotic. On a visit to an open-air swimming pool, for example, Albert confronts the typically rude, condescending attitude of Berlin petty bureaucrats, of the sort which Treichel describes in 'Berlin – Terra Incognita'. Shortly after this episode, however, Albert begins to learn about the world of illegal gambling in which Elena lives in Berlin, and himself has a disorientating encounter with a Sri Lankan transsexual in a bar. This in turn triggers more memories for Albert: specifically, his awkward visits to his mother in the 'Weserbergland', where his evasiveness about girlfriends awoke suspicions in his mother's mind about his sexuality. Such visits exposed Albert to unbearable 'Mutterdruck' (iA, 45) – as the bizarre ritual of throwing away the sandwiches which she routinely prepared for his journey back to Berlin symbolizes – and once again we see an instance of travel and of a return home ending in discomfort in Treichel's work.

Berlin also means academic study for Albert and it is clear from a number of episodes that he is making only uncertain progress with his work on Caravaggio. Treichel's parody of academic pretentiousness is sharp. The mature students at the university, for example, throw Albert's problems in travelling the world into relief. The 'Senioren' who follow the course on Caravaggio are happy travellers: 'Sie reisten bis nach Detroit, Kansas City und Hartford in Connecticut' (iA, 154) to see original Caravaggios; the contrast with Albert's ignominious adventure in Rome could hardly be greater. Albert struggles to keep up with this competition and suffers from the academic high-handedness of Professor Delbrück and his 'Assistent'. Elena's suggestion that they move together to Sardinia is therefore not just a chance for Albert to be with her on a more secure basis and to renew his affections for Italy; it also holds the promise of a new impetus to his studies:

> Sardinien! Natürlich würde er mitgehen. Seine Abschlußarbeit konnte er auf Sardinien schreiben. Er würde sein Italienisch perfektionieren. Er würde über die Universitäten von Sassari oder Cagliari Zugang zur italienischen Caravaggioliteratur haben. (iA, 177)

As we have seen already, however, travelling with high expectations is a problematic business in Treichel's work and there is a certain inevitability about the shattering of Albert's illusions once he arrives on the island. As Georg finds in *Tristanakkord*, simply getting to one's destination can be difficult and unpleasant. Albert has read about the beauty of Sardinia in a guide book, but is met by industry and ugly housing estates. Nor does Elena's house live up to his expectations, although he makes an effort to overcome his disappointment for her sake. Elena is entirely at home: she is happier than in Berlin, dresses differently, and even makes love more satisfyingly than previously. By contrast, Albert cannot integrate. He does not understand the local language and simultaneously feels excluded from and restricted by Elena's family, for all their kindness. His perception of her changes: her perfume smells different, there is a 'sardische Wehmut' (*iA*, 208) in her eyes and, albeit temporarily, she appears smaller and rounder than she did in Berlin. Klara, the appropriately named au pair whom he meets on the beach, is obviously attractive to him because she offers a connection with the clear, crisp air of north Germany and her accent even awakens a set of heavily rose-tinted childhood memories, of which there has been little evidence so far. His lust for Klara is funny in the detail which Treichel uses, but sad as far as the relationship with Elena is concerned. Only for brief moments – making love to Elena, for example, when 'ganz Sardinien verschwamm' (*iA*, 247) – is Albert able to forget where he is. Otherwise, the island interferes with his mood and his studies and the allusion to Kafka's *Die Verwandlung* – he suffers from 'ein Käfergefühl' (*iA*, 202) – confirms his overwhelming feeling of alienation. The abrupt way in which Elena breaks off during their love-making shows that she, too, has read the signs. Neither seems especially disappointed at the end of the affair but, as Albert sets off for Berlin again he does not seem to belong anywhere: 'Er sah noch nicht mal auf gute Weise norddeutsch aus' (*iA*, 256).

Throughout Treichel's prose writing, his characters' interaction with the places in which they find themselves is both a cause and a symptom of the sometimes comic, sometimes sad predicaments in which they find themselves. The essays of *Der Entwurf des Autors* show that a problematic relationship with place is a common thread in Treichel's own experiences. Memories of East Prussia, childhood in Westphalia, studies in (West) Berlin and adult travels, especially to southern Europe, represent the contours of a personal map of the world which shapes all of Treichel's prose writing. The experience which perhaps interests him most is that of the discrepancy between expectation and reality: what characters expect of a place (be it the image of the family home in East Prussia, childhood environment, or simply a destination for a day trip) and what it is actually like are repeatedly seen to be two very different things. Even the process of moving from one place to another is frequently shown to be physically discomforting and psychologically disorientating. Once Treichel's characters arrive, moreover, cultural integration into their new surroundings is often fraught with difficulty. There are linguistic barriers, even for people who can speak foreign languages, and understanding the cultural signals in a new place is a tricky business. In addition, the burden of an uncomfortable experience of a place can travel with Treichel's characters wherever they go; most obviously, the presentation of a dull and featureless childhood is common to all of his prose writing and is often used to explain his characters' problems. Just as Treichel presents his own experience of place as an uncomfortable one, so his characters are almost always out of step with where they are. This dislocation goes some way to explaining the appeal of Treichel's writing: it is the cause of much humour, but it can also lead to sad or disturbing experiences. The emotional complexity of his characters' responses to where they are and where they have been makes his work intriguing. In this sense, his characters are a series of 'wurzellos umerherirrende Menschen' and his work deals with how they succeed or fail to come to terms with this dislocation.

Notes

[1] This is Treichel's characterization of the essays in *Der Entwurf des Autors* in the interview in this volume (see p. 27).
[2] See also Chapter 6.
[3] See *EA*, 112.
[4] This episode is reworked and extended in *Der irdische Amor*.

[5] *Der Verlorene* is called 'eine Erzählung' on the dust jacket of the first edition. In the interview in this volume, Treichel himself refers to it as a novel (see p. 21).

[6] Most importantly for the logic of the fictional account, the narrator's life differs from Treichel's biography in that he knows about his missing brother from a relatively early age. The nature of the father's business is also different.

[7] See, for example, *V*, 66, 141.

[8] For a more detailed treatment of these dysfunctional patterns of behaviour and their origins, see Chapter 6.

[9] It is perhaps interesting to note that using imagery to compare the modern world to Classical myth – in order to illustrate the shortcomings of the modern – is a favourite technique of Wolfgang Koeppen, on whose work Treichel wrote his doctoral thesis. Particularly in the so-called postwar trilogy of novels, Koeppen repeatedly presents his characters as pale shadows of Classical models. See, for example, my reading of *Tauben im Gras* in *Chaos, Control and Consistency: The Narrative Vision of Wolfgang Koeppen* (Frankfurt am Main and Berne, Peter Lang, 1993).

[10] Georg reads the 'ältere Fassung' of Hölderlin's last completed 'Hymne'. The famous opening lines of this version, which Georg reads to himself, emphasize the insignificance of the human condition.

6

Guilt and Shame in Hans-Ulrich Treichel's *Der Verlorene*

DAVID CLARKE

Hans-Ulrich Treichel's *Der Verlorene* (1998) is the author's third attempt to give fictional form to his childhood experiences in prose.[1] His 'Frankfurter Poetikvorlesungen', published as *Der Entwurf des Autors* in 2000, describe Treichel's move away from poetry and towards prose writing in terms of his need to address these early years, and he speculates that it was one event in particular which provided the impetus for this change of genre in the early 1990s. It was the loss of the enclosed world of West Berlin after the fall of the Berlin Wall, a place in which Treichel felt he had achieved a provisional sense of identity,[2] which compelled him to reconsider his childhood and particularly the loss of his eldest brother, Günter, during his parents' trek from East Prussia to Westphalia in 1945 (*EA*, 46). Treichel's stated need to re-examine his parents' painful experiences in the wake of German unification appears to invite readers to regard *Der Verlorene* as a contribution to the contemporary reassessment of German suffering during the Second World War and its aftermath, and to the breaking of alleged taboos surrounding representation of that suffering.[3]

Rather than regarding his own personal reorientation after 1989 as symptomatic of a broader shift in the national psyche, however, Treichel's explanation of his own artistic and personal coming to terms with the 'Wende' operates explicitly on an individual level. As Rhys Williams has pointed out,[4] Treichel develops in his works a highly personalized perception of geography, in which his birthplace, West Berlin, France, Greece and Italy (the last three being objects of the author's 'Sehnen'[5]) fail to provide relief from the sense of 'Orientierungslosigkeit' and 'Leere' which he feels in his youth. Those locations in this list which lie outside Germany ultimately prove disappointing to Treichel, in that they fail to provide a 'Wahlheimat' for an individual who feels no sense of attachment to his own place of origin.[6] West Berlin in the 1980s, on the other hand, at least offers a geographical space in which he feels able to create his own identity through his activities as a poet. Treichel portrays the enclosed city of West Berlin as a clearly bounded space which provides the 'Splitter' of reality which he can imbue with meaning in his writing (*EA*, 41), and to which, through his poetry, he can develop 'ein starkes Heimatgefühl'.[7] Writing thus becomes a means of 'Orientierung in einem leeren Raum',[8] a process to which West Berlin appears to have been particularly conducive for Treichel during the 1980s. As the author remarks, Germany's post-war division becomes merely the backdrop to his own search for identity and a historically situated sense of belonging, a search which makes no claim to be typical or representative of his nation or of his generation:

> Die spezielle Westberliner Situation erlaubte es einem melancholischen geschichts- und beinahe ichlosen Ostwestfalen, sich lebendig und zeitgeschichtlich präsent zu fühlen. Ein hoher Preis, ließe sich einwenden: Ein ganzes Land einschließlich Hauptstadt zu halbieren und ein halbes Volk einzusperren, nur damit ein verstockter Westfale ein Geschichtsgefühl hat. Aber um eine historische Betrachtung geht es hier nicht; es geht einzig um Lebenserfahrungen und Wahrnehmungsweisen, die irgendwann in den Vorsatz münden, sich dem eigenen Selbst sowie der welt vorzugsweise schreiben zu nähern. Es geht um die Erschaffung des Autors aus dem Geist der Leere. (*EA*, 39)

The Cold War thus loses its historical significance as a geopolitical situation affecting millions, and is given an entirely personal meaning by Treichel. Unlike any traditional notion of 'Heimat', however, the identification with the city which Treichel describes cannot be shared with others: it exists within his own imagination and in the act of writing itself, so that the wider meaning of West Berlin becomes distorted from the poet's solipsistic perspective.

Treichel's need to re-examine his childhood and the experiences of his parents, particularly as regards his lost brother, indicates the fragility of the poetic project of self-creation for which West Berlin provides the geographical context. With the disappearance of West Berlin as a separate entity, Treichel feels compelled to return to his point of origin, the provincial town of Versmold, in order perhaps to assess the causes of that sense of rootlessness which plagues him and to find a new solution to his inability to belong now that West Berlin no longer exists. In doing so, however, the author discovers, through the eyes of his unnamed narrator in *Der Verlorene*, that his original 'Heimat' and his familial situation are resistant to any attempt to describe a shared historical experience which could form the basis of his identity. Although history and geography provide the context in which the figures in the text formulate their sense of self, such identities remain plural: just as in Treichel's description of pre-1989 Berlin, no common experience is discovered, only the isolation of an individual relationship to history and to place. This state of affairs can be observed most clearly in relation to the experiences of guilt and shame which are characteristic of the figures portrayed in *Der Verlorene*.

The life of the family depicted by Treichel, which is a fictionalized version of his own,[9] is dominated by these two emotions: 'Vom Tag meiner Geburt an herrschte ein Gefühl von Schuld und Scham in der Familie' (*V*, 17). It becomes apparent that these feelings are linked for his parents to their experience of their flight from East Prussia in the face of the advancing Red Army in January 1945. However, as I will demonstrate, the similarity of the feelings displayed by the parents does not necessarily point to an identical cause for their distress. For the narrator himself, these feelings are so much part of the atmosphere of his home that he comes to share them too, although for him guilt and shame are rooted in his experience of post-war family life, not in the events of 1945.

As Helen Merrell Lynd points out, commentators on the significance of guilt and shame in human psychology generally agree on the following broad definitions. Guilt, Lynd suggests, is the feeling of having broken an internalized code of conduct or morality. To experience guilt is to feel pricked by conscience at this transgression, even if the guilty individual is not called to account by others.[10] Shame, on the other hand, is an experience of incongruence between what the individual appears to be, especially in the eyes of others, and what he or she feels himself or herself to be:

> No sin has been committed. But discrepancy appears between us and the social situation, between what we feel from within and what appears to us, and perhaps to others, from without.[11]

This definition of shame is comparable, for example, to that proposed by Jean-Paul Sartre in terms of the experience of 'Being for Others', in which we feel the judgemental gaze of our fellow human beings upon us.[12] Lynd points out, however, that these two emotions, guilt and shame, are not antitheses; rather, the distinction is a question of emphasis. Furthermore, the two feelings can overlap, as is clearly the case for the family portrayed in *Der Verlorene*.[13] In order to show the interaction between shame and guilt in the lives of the narrator and his parents in Treichel's text I will treat them individually, outlining the separate origins of these feelings in each figure.

The notion of guilt in West German society in the post-war period obviously carries with it connotations relating to the crimes perpetrated in the name of the German people by the National Socialist regime. Although we are told little about the lives of the parents before their flight from East Prussia, we do know that they harboured resentments against their Polish neighbours and identified with the National Socialist denigration of Poles and Russians as inferior beings: this becomes particularly apparent during the father's conversation with Professor Liebstedt (*V*, 110–11). Nevertheless, this possible ideological identification with Nazism does not lead to a sense of responsibility for the crimes of Hitler's regime, since the parents tend to focus their attention on their own suffering at the hands of Russian troops in 1945. This neglect of the suffering of the victims of National Socialism, Albrecht Lehmann has argued, was typical of the attitudes of many expellees in the immediate post-war period, who were vociferous in their opposition to any expressions of German guilt precisely because of the scale of their own loss.[14]

For the narrator's father, guilt is connected to his abandonment of his farm in Rakowiec, in violation of a personal moral code which links the farmer to the land he cultivates and confers upon him a responsibility not to leave it. Despite his success in business in post-war Westphalia, he still regards himself as 'ein Bauer aus Rakowiec' (for example, *V*, 86) who has 'sinned' because he left his house of his own free will: 'Ein Bauer aus Rakowiec verläßt sein Haus nicht freiwillig. Wer sein Haus verläßt, versündigt sich' (*V*, 122). In the context of the final weeks of the Second World War, it may seem curious for the father to feel guilty for leaving his farm, especially given the dangers of staying in East Prussia. It might be

Guilt and Shame in Der Verlorene

argued that the parents of the narrator are 'Flüchtlinge' rather than 'Vertriebene' in the purest sense of the term, since they left their home out of fear of the advancing Red Army, rather than being forcibly ejected by the Polish authorities after the end of the war, when Poland gained former German territory east of the Oder-Neisse Line. In this sense, it might be possible for the father to feel that he has abandoned his land rather than being forced to leave, especially since, as Louis Ferdinand Helbig observes, the Soviet and Polish authorities did make use of the fact that many Germans had fled territories such as East Prussia in order to help justify their confiscation of these lands from Germany.[15] Nevertheless, both 'Flüchtlinge' and 'Vertriebene' were treated equally by the authorities of the Federal Republic in terms of compensation, and all were classified under the latter category; a reasonable conclusion, since even those who left before the beginning of expulsions would not have been allowed to return permanently to their homes.[16] It therefore seems anomalous that the narrator's father in *Der Verlorene* should continue to feel a sense of guilt for having left his land, given that, objectively, he had little choice. However, it is his subjective sense of having transgressed his deeply held principles which explains his continuing sense of guilt after the war, not any feeling of responsibility for crimes perpetrated by Germany during the conflict.

The narrator's mother also feels guilty for actions carried out at a moment of crisis for which she cannot objectively be held responsible. In her case, she feels that she has done wrong by having given away Arnold, the narrator's disappeared elder sibling, to another woman on the trek. This act was motivated by her fear that the Russian soldiers she and her husband had just encountered were about to kill the family. This misapprehension is founded to a large extent on her racist belief that the Russians are murderous barbarians, but she comes to realize after the fact that, despite her rape by the soldiers, she need never have abandoned her child: 'sie habe voreilig Angst um ihr eigenes Leben und das Leben ihres Kindes gehabt, und in Wahrheit habe sie das Kind voreilig weggegeben' (*V*, 16). In this sense, rather than both parents bearing 'eine gewisse Schuld für [Arnolds] Verschwinden', as Achim Nuber suggests, this guilt is perceived by the mother as belonging to herself alone.[17]

The parallel between these two different losses, and between the two distinct yet comparable senses of guilt which they provoke, can be seen in the comparison which the narrator makes between his parents' struggle to identify 'Findelkind 2307' as Arnold and their fight for material restitution. Towards the end of the text, we learn that the narrator's father has been denied payments under the compensation scheme ('Lastenausgleich') set up by the Federal Government in 1952, 'wegen der Rechtslage' (V, 163).[18] The reasons for this remain unclear, yet the mother identifies what she sees as a clear link between this perceived injustice and the refusal of the authorities to recognize her as the mother of 'Findelkind 2307', alias the butcher's apprentice Heinrich. She feels that she is being 'noch einmal beraubt' (V, 163) and once again treated unjustly (V, 163-4). I would suggest here that the parents of the narrator wish to have their individual senses of guilt assuaged by an official confirmation that they have in fact been the unwilling victims of injustice, rather than having to live with what they perceive to be their active role in their own loss. Compensation for what they secretly believe they gave away would relieve them of responsibility by recognizing them entirely as injured parties.

Although the father is closely involved in the search for Arnold, it is clearly the mother who is the driving force behind this project. It is her unhappiness which pushes the father to explore every possible avenue in order to find Arnold again, yet he plays a secondary role. This can be explained by the fact that his particular sense of guilt is related, as I have argued above, to his abandonment of his farm in East Prussia, for which he now knows he will not be compensated. He consequently develops an alternative strategy for dealing with his guilt in the creation of a new and successful life as a businessman in the post-war Federal Republic. The expansion of his business represents a gradual overcoming of his loss which slowly erases any traces of his former life from his present situation. Initially, he is unable to relax, despite the fact that he has built up a new 'Existenz' through his business (V, 45), and he therefore sets about converting his house into a modern shop. The rebuilding of this 'Fachwerkhaus', with its echoes of a rural past, destroys an apparently unreachable room into which the narrator peers as a child through a trap door. This 'verborgen[e] Raum' (V, 48) functions as a metaphor for the father's former life, to which the child does not have access and which the father wishes to cover over, even if, as the narrator claims, it continues to be somehow present after it has ceased to exist physically (*V*, 48). This rebuilding continues later with the construction of a storage facility for the father's new wholesale business. This finally necessitates the destruction of old farm buildings which, the narrator surmises, the father has left untouched up to this point for sentimental reasons: 'er hatte sie in dem Zustand gelassen, in dem er sie vorgefunden hatte, und dies wohl auch, weil sie ihn an seine bäuerliche Vergangenheit in Rakowiec erinnerten' (*V*, 76). Significantly, the father's decision to undertake this latter piece of building work is motivated not only by his desire for 'Umsatzsteigerung' (*V*, 75), but also by the failure of the first set of scientific examinations paid for by the parents to establish that 'Findelkind 2307' is their son. By increasing his status in the business world, he hopes to distance himself from the past and demonstrate that he has overcome his loss, especially in those moments when his wife's obsession with finding her child threatens to identify him again with his former existence.

The father's attempts to move on and establish himself in the role of a successful small businessman can be seen not just in terms of his desire to make up for the material loss which the 'Lastenausgleich' failed to address, and thus free himself from his guilt over his abandonment of his farm in East Prussia, but also as a means of avoiding shame. As I have already suggested, shame can be explained as a feeling of discomfort caused by a discrepancy between the self-image of the individual and the perceptions and expectations of others. In the case of the father, he clearly has a strong attachment to his former identity as an East Prussian farmer, yet he feels compelled to conceal this identity from the outside world, as his conversion of the buildings discussed above demonstrates. He indulges in the rituals of his former homeland, such as in the 'Schweinehirnessen' which so disgusts his son, but these moments of true contentment and ease can only be enjoyed in private with other expellees. During these meals, he becomes 'heiter' and 'ausgelassen' (*V*, 43), yet these feelings give way by the end of the evening to a painful silence: 'Und fast immer endeten die Essensabende damit, daß irgendwann auch der Vater und die Gäste zuerst nur noch leise und schließlich gar nicht miteinander sprachen' (*V*, 45). The father feels he must do penance for slipping back into his old identity, and throws himself with even more energy into his business the next day (*V*, 45).

Lehmann suggests that expellees felt a particular pressure towards economic success in the 1960s, as such material advancement was interpreted as a sign of integration into the society of the economic miracle.[19] This is certainly the case for the narrator's father in *Der Verlorene*, who exerts himself to a life-threatening extent in order to preserve an outward image of himself as an ever more prosperous member of West German society. The more and more expensive cars which his wealth allows him to buy are primarily a means of demonstrating the family's material success to the world and, therefore, their belonging in West Germany: as the narrator observes, 'er glaubte, [. . .] die Familie damit auszeichnen zu können' (*V*, 80).

The gap between the father's genuine self and his persona as a businessman is no more apparent than in the scene in which the narrator sees his father's mismatched feet for the first time during the family's examination by Professor Liebstedt's assistant. Clothing, for the father, is an important means of demonstrating his new identity as a prosperous West German. The prospect of meeting such an illustrious person as Liebstedt, which is not the sort of thing 'ein Bauer aus Rakowiec' expects to do (*V*, 86), unsettles him until he is dressed by his wife, who helps him into clothes which signify his new, self-confident, West German identity:

> Sie machte aus dem Bauern einen Geschäftsmann, und dieser verlor erst dann wieder etwas von seiner Unruhe und Unsicherheit, als er im korrekten grauen Anzug, mit Mantel und Hut auf die Straße trat und mir und der Mutter mit festen Schritten in Richtung Gerichtslaboratorium vorausging. (*V*, 87)

As the narrator observes, the father appears not to be made of flesh and blood, which metaphorically signifies his true identity, but rather of 'gestärkten Hemden, einem Anzug mit Weste und Lederhandschuhen' (*V*, 89). His true self is, like his feet, something grotesque which must be hidden from the gaze of the world around him.

The adoption of an external persona which is ultimately incompatible with the true self of the individual and the insecurity, embarrassment and shame which mark those moments in which the discrepancy between the two threatens to become recognizable to the outside world are mainstays of Treichel's humour in *Der Verlorene* and elsewhere. The father portrayed in *Heimatkunde*, for example, is comparable with the father of the narrator of *Der Verlorene*, in that he adopts the role of a tobacconist and the heavy smoking habit which is an essential part of this identity as a means of improving his business prospects: 'Ein nichtrauchender Tabakwarenhändler, das sei wie ein vegetarischer Fleischer. Wohl rauche er gern, aber er rauche aus geschäftlichen Gründen' (H, 27). The father is compared unfavourably with the 'Helden des Rauchens' who visit his shop and who inspire a sense of 'Bewunderung' in the narrator as a child (H, 28). Whilst the father is only playing a role, being a smoker is an essential part of the identity of these figures, who attain a perversely heroic status by continuing to smoke even when they have been forbidden to do so by their doctors and have to suffer amputations and incapacitation as a result of their addiction. As in *Der Verlorene*, however, the father in *Heimatkunde* hides his true self beneath his clothing, which is described in great detail as stiff and constricting (H, 20–1).

The visit of the 'Negerpastor' to the small town, described in the same volume, offers another example of this comedy of identity. During the course of an evening spent in the house of the narrator's parents, it becomes clear that the visiting African clergyman is the cultural superior of the local German pastor, who entered the church with little formal training after the Second World War. The frustration of the family's expectations of an African, who turns out to have a doctorate and to speak a number of languages, is juxtaposed with the clear discomfort of their own pastor, who finds his ignorance and his inadequacy in relation to his official role exposed in public. The narrator himself suffers a similarly embarrassing exposure in *Heimatkunde*, when his skills as a poet are found wanting in the translation of a Portuguese poem into German (H, 111–23). Knowing that none of the participants in the seminar he is attending speak fluent German, he believes that he can get away with substituting the word 'Darre' for 'Dürre' in order to make his translation rhyme. However, he is then confronted with a late arrival, a professional translator of Portuguese poetry into German, who immediately sees through this ruse. Faced with the translator's laughter and his own humiliation, he has no option but to leave the building without a word. This experience of artistic failure is shared with Georg in the novel *Tristanakkord* (2000), who plagiarizes freely from Georg Heym, yet is quickly exposed by the composer Bergmann, who has commissioned him to write the poem (*T*, 231). As Georg's recollections of his adolescence demonstrate, this feeling of having failed to live up to the image of himself as an artist that he would like project to those around him does not even require the direct gaze of the other in order to produce a sense of shame. His dream of becoming a rock musician, for example, is abandoned when he is confronted with the self which is perceived by the outside world in a mirror as he pretends to play the guitar. He realizes at this point that others will not see in him a 'strahlenden Gittarenvirtuosen', but only 'einen etwas zu dick geratenen pubertären Knaben, blaß, verschwitzt und ungelenk', and covers the mirror so as to avoid this sight (*T*, 29).

In *Der Verlorene*, the family outings which the narrator is forced to endure on Sundays are a particular moment of shame which conforms with the pattern outlined above. These trips are 'wahre Schuld- und Schamprozessionen' (*V*, 19), which are ruined in some way, the narrator infers, by the memory of what happened to his brother Arnold (*V*, 20). On one level, his parents may feel guilty for enjoying themselves after having committed their respective misdeeds. However, it is significant that their destination on these journeys can also be interpreted, like the father's efforts to sustain his image as a successful West German businessman, as an attempt to demonstrate their integration into their new homeland. The excursions take in the local landmarks of the 'Teutoberger Wald' and the 'Bismarckturm', the latter which they climb in order to admire the view across the plain to their 'Heimatort' (*V*, 19).[20] These visits take on the function of pilgrimages which proclaim the family's identification with their new homeland, yet this attempt to make a public display of their integration masks the guilt they feel at having abandoned both their true 'Heimat' and, in the mother's case, their first child. It is the knowledge of this discrepancy between their true feelings and their desire to project an entirely different picture of themselves to the society in which they now live which, I would argue, is the source of the shame which accompanies their guilt.

The narrator's mother's sense of shame is arguably also founded upon a mismatch between what she perceives herself to be and the image she feels forced to live up to. She is initially less successful in dealing with her sense of guilt, in that she has not given up on the hope of restitution of her loss, which would free her from her feelings of having transgressed her own moral code. This morality is less clearly delineated in the text than are the father's beliefs about what is right and wrong for 'ein Bauer aus Rakowiec', yet it is clearly linked to her views on what is appropriate and inappropriate behaviour for a wife and mother. The counterpart to the father's business activities in the mother's life is housework, which, the narrator states, is a means for her to fight her sense of guilt and shame:

> Je mehr sich die Mutter im Haus zu schaffen machte, um so weniger konnten die Scham und Schuld sich ihrer bemächtigen. Und in Wahrheit tat die Mutter nichts anderes, als sich im Haus zu schaffen zu machen. Ebenso wie der Vater nichts anderes tat, als sich um die Geschäfte zu kümmern. (V, 32)

By occupying herself entirely with the traditional duties of the wife and mother, she seeks, I would argue, to atone for what she regards as the dereliction of those duties in carelessly giving away her child. Her sense of shame can equally be combated in this way, as she is able to demonstrate to the outside world that she is fully committed to this conventional role, even though she secretly feels that she has failed to live up to its demands. This is also evident when the results of the first 'erbbiologisches Gutachten' fail to establish that she is the birth mother of 'Findelkind 2307'. Here she seeks to exhibit her capacity to love as a mother, which she otherwise generally fails to show in relation to her second child, by embracing him so hard that he feels 'in den Bauch der Mutter hineingedrückt' (V, 74). In this way, she tries to prove her conformity to a stereotypical conception of motherhood, although she is haunted by the belief that her previous actions call that conformity into question. This interpretation of the mother's shame adds a further dimension to her feelings during the weekend excursions already discussed above, a ritual which also demonstrates to the outside world that mother, father and son form an intact family unit, thereby obscuring the fact that the mother believes herself to have betrayed her duties to the family in the past.

It can be argued, therefore, that the parents' experiences of the end of the Second World War, although both understandable in terms of comparable processes of guilt and shame, are very different from each other in terms of the origins of their feelings. This accounts for the pervasive lack of communication in the parental household, as can be seen, for example, in the mother's silence during the 'Schweinehirnessen' or by her burning of the pile of money which the father intends to use to buy a new car (*V*, 45, 82). Whilst the narrator shares the parents' guilt and shame, he cannot logically feel himself responsible for the actions which led to these feelings, since he was not yet born at the time. Consequently, his case also helps to demonstrate that apparently similar emotional reactions to historical circumstances are, in fact, highly individual.

The psychology of the narrator of Treichel's *Der Verlorene* is perhaps the most difficult aspect of the text. Although he is capable of some insight in relation to his parents, his own feelings of guilt and shame are not analysed, since he only rarely makes use of a more knowing, adult perspective, preferring to represent his confused adolescent feelings directly. From the point of view of the formulation of his own identity, however, his central problem is his inability to see his place within the family and its history as the foundation of his own sense of self. The chief difficulty for the narrator is that any attempt to define himself in such terms would be equivalent to a negation of his own existence. In the family's perception of its situation, he has usurped the place of Arnold, the good, lost son, and is an ungrateful and selfish child, insensitive to his parents' loss, as his father complains at one point (*V*, 48–9). In his mother's eyes, he has no identity in his own right, but is rather 'nur das, was sie verloren hatte' (*V*, 140). In fact, her only real communication with him seems to take place when examining photographs of Arnold or discussing Arnold's fate (for example, *V*, 12). His sense of guilt, therefore, can be best explained in terms of the belief that is imposed upon him, through his internalization of his parents' attitudes, that he has committed an offence by his very existence, which is presented to him as an intrusion into the family which Arnold would have made complete.

As other commentators have pointed out, the 'Nebenrolle' (*V*, 17) assigned to the narrator within the family is demonstrated most clearly in the family photo album.[21] Here Arnold's picture, which shows him as a baby lying on a white wool blanket in a photographer's studio, takes a central place, whereas the narrator's body appears only in fragments on small amateur shots which are relegated to the back of the album (V, 7–9). Arnold's photograph, which is contrasted with the 'nur teilweise Anwesenheit' of the narrator in the album (V, 9), allows the absent elder child to appear more real and present than the narrator, since, as Roland Barthes has argued of photography in general, its 'essence is to ratify what it represents', providing incontrovertible proof of the historical existence of the narrator's brother.[22] It seems paradoxical, in light of his experience of the negation of his self in the photo album, that the narrator should resent his father's decision that he too should finally be photographed by a professional photographer as his brother was before him. In one sense, his resistance to this notion can be explained by the fact that these photographs are only designed to be 'brauchbar' (V, 64) in terms of the parents' search for Arnold, and thus do nothing to help the narrator secure his sense of belonging in the family. At the same time, however, being photographed is regarded by the narrator as a process of being 'bloßgestellt' (V, 65). The individuals displayed in the pictures outside the photographer's shop are confirmands, young couples, brides and bridegrooms, and young families with their children, representing the rites of passage of the conventional family. Yet, for the narrator, the family has become not the sphere in which identity is secured and affirmed, but rather the sphere in which it is denied, so that he associates these photographs with death (V, 65). The fact that his father orders him to have his hair cut to 'Lagerinsassenhaarlänge' for the purpose (V, 68), recalling the inmates of Nazi concentration camps, adds a further deathly dimension to the photographs which are eventually taken of him.

The parents' search for Arnold generally contributes to the narrator's own sense of not belonging in the family. As the various tests and examinations take their course, evidence mounts that, not only is 'Findelkind 2307' unlikely to be the child of his parents, but also that there is no conclusive reason to believe that the narrator is definitely related to them either (V, 61, 151). Eventually, he speculates that he might in fact be related to 'Findelkind 2307', but not to his parents, or that he might be a 'Russenkind', perhaps referring subconsciously here to the rape of his mother by Russian soldiers (V, 151).

This sense of being in some way an interloper or impostor within a family to which he does not truly belong helps to explain the narrator's experience of shame. When being examined by Professor Liebstedt and his assistant, for example, the narrator is tortured by 'Scham und Verlegenheit' (V, 95, 115), which can be interpreted as his reaction to the attempts of the medical personnel to document the nature of his biological relationship with his family. Here the reader again sees that gap between the self-perception of the subject and the expectations of the outside world: the narrator does not feel part of the family to which, from the perspective of others, he should belong, and suspects that he might not be their biological offspring. The supposedly scientific tests which are designed to establish the parentage of 'Findelkind 2307' hold the potential, as the results later show, to reveal his status as an intruder and impostor, exposing his inability to be a good and legitimate son. His other experiences of embarrassment and shame can be seen in similar terms. Whilst the feelings provoked by watching 'Intimitäten' on the television screen with his mother present, described in terms of 'Verlegengheit' and 'Beschämung' (V, 31), can be regarded as typical of those of a pubescent boy, the reference to sex and biology in these images highlights those forces which allow a child to enter into the family and which, as the scientific tests undergone by the narrator and his parents emphasize, establish his or her belonging in that family. Later, at his father's funeral, he is ashamed of the black armband he is required to wear, since he can feel no grief for his father's death: 'Ich wollte ein guter und trauriger Sohn sein, und ich dachte daran, daß ich wohl unter dem Tod des Vaters litt, aber nicht spürte, daß ich litt' (V, 138). This failure to live up to expectations of what 'ein guter Sohn' should be extends to his reaction to his mother's grief, whose embrace also makes him 'verlegen' (V, 133). He can feel no sense of identification with his family, since their own attitudes to him have made him feel like an intruder who has taken the place of their beloved Arnold, yet they also have the clear expectation that he will demonstrate his love for them as a son. This discrepancy between what his parents, and indeed the rest of society, require of him and his own true feelings is the ultimate source of this sense of shame.

This interpretation of the narrator's shame goes some way to explaining his surprising identification with Heinrich, the adopted 'Findelkind 2307' at the very end of the text. It has been suggested that the mother's inability to recognize Heinrich as the older double of the narrator may be attributable to the fact that it is only the narrator who imagines this likeness.²³ Alternatively, Tabener argues, the mother's final rejection of Heinrich may be symbolic of her wish to 'begin a new life [. . .] unburdened by the past' with Herr Rudolf.²⁴ The narrator's desire to be identical with Heinrich, however, whether based on a distorted perception or not, is indicative of his desire for a genuine sense of belonging based on biological ties. His identification of Heinrich as his 'um einige Jahre älteres Spiegelbild' (V, 174) holds out the prospect of a familial relationship which will not be characterized by shame: if he is clearly and demonstrably related to Heinrich, then he will be able to experience a sense of belonging which is not called into question by his own belief that he is somehow an interloper or a fake. Whereas earlier in the novel he is afflicted with muscular spasms in the face which are designed to deny this physical similarity (V, 57-8), he now sees in his resemblance to Heinrich an alternative to the shameful situation of only pretending to be the good and rightful son which he does not feel himself to be. Finally, however, this liberation is denied to the narrator, which is an ironic move on Treichel's part, given that elsewhere he presents his childhood in prose fiction as a renewed quest for identity after the collapse of the artificial 'Heimat' of West Berlin. To judge on the basis of *Der Verlorene*, Treichel apparently ends by rejecting this past as the starting point for a reformulation of his personal sense of belonging.

In my examination of experiences of guilt and shame in Treichel's *Der Verlorene*, I have demonstrated that these emotional states are essentially polyvalent. Despite the common psychological mechanisms apparently at work here, the experiences which lead to feelings of guilt and shame for the three main figures in the text are fundamentally heterogeneous. Although the mother and father appear to share a sense of common guilt and shame, which originates in the final months of the Second World War and in the demands of West German society, this apparent unity masks highly individual concerns. The socio-historical context which allows these different feelings of guilt and shame to grow may be the same, but their characteristics can be clearly distinguished. This is just as much the case, if not more so, for the narrator, whose guilt and shame arise from a very peculiar family situation. In this sense, whilst Treichel sees his story as an example of 'transgenerationellen Traumatisierung',²⁵ suggesting a single origin for the guilt and shame suffered by both the parents and their child, the roots of these feelings in the narrator's experience are as individual and, one might even say, eccentric as the author's own perception of the Cold War and its effects on Germany.

This individualization of guilt and shame is the true provocation of Treichel's text. Set against that discourse of German guilt and shame which, as Mary Fulbrook argues, dominated the West German state's official self-presentation,[26] Treichel's *Der Verlorene* suggests that even those individuals who appeared to share in this 'culture of public anguish' may, in fact, have been motivated by private concerns which 'could not be easily integrated into the official story of ritual guilt and mourning' for the crimes committed by Germans under the National Socialist regime.[27] Such emotions are thus called into question as a means by which a unified national response to history might be constructed. Moreover, history itself is presented in *Der Verlorene* as it is experienced on an individual basis, frustrating attempts to formulate a grand narrative of the past or a shared attitude to that past which could serve as a basis for national identity.

Notes

[1] The volumes *Von Leib und Seele* (1992) and *Heimatkunde oder Alles ist heiter und edel* (1996) also contain episodes based on Treichel's childhood.

[2] See Treichel's poem 'Halbes Liebeslied für Berlin': 'Hier lebe ich halb/Woanders wäre ich tot'. Treichel, *Gespräch unter Bäumen. Gedichte* (Frankfurt am Main, Suhrkamp Taschenbuch, 2002), 100.

[3] W. G. Sebald's essay *Literatur und Luftkrieg* (Munich, Hanser, 1999), for example, famously calls for a breaking of the taboo which the author claims exists in German literature in relation to the bombing of German cities by British and American planes. More recently, Günter Grass's *Im Krebsgang* (Göttingen, Steidl, 2002), which depicts the catastrophic sinking of the passenger ship *Wilhelm Gustloff* at the end of the Second World War, has been widely received as an attempt to give representation to German suffering which had previously been silenced. Stuart Tabener has convincingly argued that it is inappropriate to read Treichel's text in these terms (Tabener, 'Hans-Ulrich Treichel's *Der Verlorene* and the problem of German wartime suffering', *Modern Language Review*, 97/1 (2002), 123–34). Nevertheless, Hans-Ludwig Arnold's review of *Der Verlorene* reads the

book in this context as 'die genaue und sensible Erkundung eines bislang weitgehend tabuisierten Erzählterrains' (Arnold, 'Auf der Suche nach Arnold', *Der Spiegel*, 22 March 1998, 244).

[4] Rhys W. Williams, '"Mein unbewusstes . . . kannte den Fall der Mauer und die deutsche Wiedervereinigung nicht"': the writer Hans-Ulrich Treichel', *German Life and Letters*, 55/2 (2002), 208–18.

[5] See the chapters 'Geographie des Sehnens' and 'Rom oder die Mittagsdämonen', in *EA*.

[6] This is a disappointment which Treichel shares in relation to Italy with Albert, the protagonist of *Der irdische Amor*.

[7] Heinz Blumensath, '"Lebenstationen" – Heinz Blumensath im Gespräch mit Hans-Ulrich Treichel', *Glossen*, 7 (1999).

[8] Ibid.

[9] Treichel's parents lived in the same village of Rakowiec in East Prussia as the parents of his narrator. The main difference between his childhood and that portrayed in *Der Verlorene* is that Treichel's parents did not inform their children about their search for their lost eldest son until shortly before Treichel's mother's death (see *EA*, 16–30). Certain details, such as Treichel's other siblings and his father's loss of an arm in the First World War, are omitted, although they are included in his other autobiographical fictions.

[10] Helen Merrell Lynd, *On Shame and the Search for Identity* (New York, Harvest, 1958), 21 and 23.

[11] Ibid., 23. For a similar use of the notions of guilt and shame, see Ruth Benedict's comparison of Japanese and American society, where she describes the former as a 'culture of shame' and the latter as a 'culture of guilt' (Benedict, *The Chrysanthemum and the Sword: Patterns of Japanese Culture* (Cambridge, Mass., Riverside Press, 1946), 223).

[12] Jean-Paul Sartre, *Being and Nothingness: An Essay in Phenomenological Ontology*, trans. Hazel E. Barnes (London, Routledge, 1969, originally 1943), 261.

[13] Lynd, *On Shame*, 23.

[14] Albrecht Lehmann, *Im Fremden ungewollt zuhaus. Flüchtlinge und Vertriebene in Westdeutschland, 1945–1990* (Munich, Beck, 1991), 241.

[15] Louis Ferdinand Helbig, *Der ungeheure Verlust. Flucht und Vertreibung in der deutschsprachigen Belletristik der Nachkriegszeit*, 3rd edn (Wiesbaden, Harrasowitz, 1996), 175.

[16] Although around one million refugees did return home after the end of the fighting, they were later expelled. Klaus-Dietmar Henke, 'Der Weg nach Potsdam – Die Alliierten und die Vertreibung', in Wolfgang Benz (ed.), *Die Vertreibung aus dem Osten. Ursachen, Ereignisse, Folgen* (Frankfurt am Main, Fischer Taschenbuch, 1995), 58–85 (79).

[17] Arnold Nuber, 'Kindheit und Jugend im Zeichen von Flucht und Vertreibung. Hans-Ulrich Treichels *Der Verlorene* im Kontext zeitgenössischer Biographieerzählungen', in Sascha Feuchert (ed.), *Flucht und Vertreibung in der deutschen Literatur. Beiträge* (Frankfurt am Main, Lang, 2001), 265– 80 (273).

[18] For details of the 'Lastenausgleich', see Reinhold Schillinger, 'Der Lastenausgleich', in Benz (ed.), *Die Vertreibung*, 231–43.

[19] Lehmann, *Im Fremden*, 69.

[20] The inability to identify with and be proud of landmarks which are supposed to inspire a sense of local patriotism is also the subject of the story 'Heimatkunde' (Treichel, *H*, 47–57).

[21] See, for example, Tabener, 'Treichel's *Der Verlorene*', 127 and Harald Jähner, 'Aufstrebende Flügelrandabschweifung', *Berliner Zeitung*, 25 April 1998.

[22] Roland Barthes, *Camera Lucida*, trans. Richard Howard (London, Vintage, 2000, originally 1980), 85.

[23] Nuber, 'Kindheit und Jugend', 275.

[24] Tabener, 'Treichel's *Der Verlorene*', 134.

[25] Rhys W. Williams, '"Leseerfahrungen sind Lebenserfahrungen": Gespräch mit Hans-Ulrich Treichel', p. 11 in this volume.

[26] Mary Fulbrook, *German National Identity after the Holocaust* (Cambridge, Polity, 1999), 20.

[27] Ibid., 166–7.

7

'sehnsüchtig-traurig und unerlöst': Memory's Longing to Forget. Or Why *Tristanakkord* is not Simply a Reprise of Martin Walser

STUART TABERNER

Christoph Bartmann perhaps succinctly captures the sentiments of the majority of reviewers when he describes Hans-Ulrich Treichel's novelistic efforts as fixing a 'Poetik der Schüchternheit'.[1] Nor is this critic alone in uncovering affinities between Treichel and Kafka, or, still more frequently, beween Treichel and Thomas Bernhard and Martin Walser. Ulrike Baureithel accordingly identifies a 'typisch Treichelschen, an Bernhard gemahnenden Duktus', including a preference for 'indirekte, lakonische Rede',[2] whilst Ina Hartwig detects Bernhard's impact more readily in the 'Neigung zur komischen Überhöhung' and the 'Rhythmik gezielter Wiederholung und Übertreibungen'.[3] Martin Ebel, moreover, perceives both the 'gnadenlose Konsequenz eines Thomas Bernhards' as well as 'die Produktivität des Scheiterns, wie wir sie von Martin Walser kennen'.[4] With specific reference to the novel *Tristanakkord* (2000), Tilman Krause adds to the list and claims that the book's kinship with the *Künstlerroman* 'fordert den Vergleich mit Goethe und Keller, mit Novalis, Eichendorff und Thomas Mann heraus'.[5]

That Treichel should allude to a wide range of authors is scarcely surprising, of course. He is, after all, a professor of German literature at an institute dedicated to fostering creative writing. He has published widely in academic and journalistic contexts on Koeppen (his *Doktorarbeit*), Kafka, Robert Walser, Peter Weiss, Ernst Jünger, Arno Schmidt and Enzensberger (some of these essays are collated in *Über die Schrift hinaus. Essays zur Literatur*, 2000), as well as Georg Trakl, Gottfried Benn, Wolfgang Hildesheimer and Günter Eich, amongst others, and contemporary authors Peter Handke, W. G. Sebald, Ludwig Harig, Fritz Rudolf Fries and Ingo Schramm. He has also written reviews of Italian, French and Swedish authors. A particular interest has been modern American writing, including James Salter, T. C. Boyle, Anne Tyler and Colum McCann. This perhaps accounts for the quality of readability and storytelling that may strike readers as typical of recent Anglo-American fiction. In any event, the author's intertextual borrowings are, as might be expected, almost always foregrounded in a distinctly self-conscious manner.

As well as situating Treichel's debt to other writers, both contemporary and canonical, critics have also been keen to locate autobiographical elements in his texts. Once again, Treichel has scarcely concealed the manner in which his own history has fed into the plot-lines of his two novels, *Der Verlorene* (1998) and *Tristanakkord*. Two earlier volumes of essays, *Von Leib und Seele* (1992) and *Heimatkunde oder Alles ist heiter und edel* (1996) thus detail with laconic dexterity the author's strained yet obsessive relationship with his 'ostwestfälischen Heimat' (*H*, 47–57), his parents' experience of fleeing the Russians at the end of the war, and the story of the older brother 'lost' on the trek, which is reworked in *Der Verlorene* as an investigation into the attitude of the generation of 1968 towards German suffering in the Second World War.[6] This trauma, moreover, is retold in an article for the *Neue Züricher Zeitung*, 'Lektionen der Leere. Eine Kindheit auf dem Lande. Oder wie ich Schriftsteller wurde', which was published in April 2000.[7] In each case, the defining themes are: provinciality, the absence of any family narrative of a shared past, the emptiness of childhood memories, lack of confidence and reticence.

Many of these autobiographical elements are present in *Tristanakkord*, a novel which Bartmann describes as 'die Fortsetzung des Verlorenen'.[8] The acutely insecure protagonist, Georg, hails from the backwater Emsfelde, endures childhood as a period of numbing emptiness, and is alienated from his father, an ex-soldier with a prosthetic arm (similar, of course, to Treichel's own father and the father-figure in *Der Verlorene*). In addition, Georg is engaged in doctoral research into the motif of *Vergessen in der Literatur*, a detail which allows Treichel to reflect self-consciously, and certainly comically, on the futility of secondary literature! At the same time, however, and as a result of a sequence of coincidences, Georg is employed by the composer Bergmann to proof-read his memoirs, an assignment which requires him to follow the distinguished artist first to Scotland, then to New York and Sicily. Georg is in awe of the maestro's many accomplishments and correspondingly aware of his own inadequacy. The narrator's 'lapidarer Tonfall', to cite Jeanette Stickler, resting on an 'artifizielle Umständlichkeit der Sprache, die Übergenauigkeit in der Beobachtung', ruthlessly exposes this insufficiency.[9] Yet neither is Bergmann spared. He is presented as the most hypocritical kind of elitist: a snob who despises the mass entertainment industry but who rushes to appear on chat shows, manufactures press conferences and revels in his popular success. The narrator's comic portrayal of the artist reveals to the reader the bullying conceit that the consistently naive Georg fails to spot. This depiction, too, also has an autobiographical source. Bergmann's hostility to his rival Nerlinger no doubt draws on Treichel's experience of writing libretti for Hans Werner Henze, whose difficult relationship with fellow composer Karlheinz Stockhausen is well known.

As Martin Bauer reminds us in timely fashion, the use of autobiographical elements in itself 'besagt nichts'. What counts is the manner in which Treichel fictionalizes personal biography such that it takes on more extensive applicability: 'Geschickt kolportiert der Lyriker und Erzähler Versatzstücke seiner eigenen Biografie, stellt sie in neue Zusammenhänge und durchlöchert sie mit Fiktion.'[10] Autobiography is externalized and generalized. It is perhaps this aspect, and the way in which perceived autobiographical failure and personal inadequacy are transformed into an ironic vision of the social universe, that align Treichel's fiction more closely with that of Martin Walser than with any other of his influences.

Certainly, there is much in *Tristanakkord* in particular that recalls Walser. Ina Hartwig notes 'das Aufeinanderprallen des kleinbürgerlichen, verklemmten Banalität Georgs auf der einen Seite und der künstlerisch-geniehaften Exzentrizität Bergmanns auf der anderen Seite',[11] a description that could just as easily describe the tension at the heart of Walser novels from *Ehen in Philippsburg* (1957) to *Ein springender Brunnen* (1998). Andrea Köhler's characterization of Treichel's Georg as belonging to 'einer aussterbenden Art: den Schamhaften',[12] moreover, could apply equally to Walser's figures, especially in his Kristlein trilogy (1960–73), who appear as relics left over from an innocent age of modest self-effacement now destroyed by the confessional self-display of the culture industry.[13] In similar fashion, Martin Ebel's allusion to 'die Produktivität des Scheiterns, wie wir sie von Martin Walser kennen',[14] already cited above, describes well the obsession with the individual's failure to assert his (these figures are invariably male) subjectivity in the face of objective, that is, seemingly inalterable, circumstances.

Treichel has also recorded how he was 'in gewisser Weise auf [Walsers] *Gallistl'sche Krankheit* geprägt'. Above all, it seems, the author was impressed by the way in which Walser's protagonist yearns for confirmation of his self-image – Treichel quotes Gallistl: 'Eine Zeitlang hoffte ich, irgend jemand werde sich der Meinung, die ich von mir habe, anschliessen' – and his sense of being persecuted by his own thoughts: 'Tagelang geht mir alles, was ich nicht aushalten kann, durch den Kopf.'[15] This obstinate fascination with neurotic navel-gazing and the disjuncture between self-image and projected image coalesce into the debilitating mix of 'Selbstreflexion und Schamhaftigkeit' diagnosed for Georg by Köhler.[16] Georg, in addition, would almost certainly endorse the following elucidation by Walser, published in a slim volume revealingly entitled *Über die Schüchternheit* (1999): 'Schüchternheit, ein anderes Wort für Sehnsucht'.[17] In similar fashion, both Treichel and Walser tend to describe characters who long to quit the province for the wider world, hoping to achieve success and even fame there. This applies to Hans Beumann in Walser's *Ehen in Philippsburg*, to the author's Anselm Kristlein in the 1960s, and characters in his novels of the 1970s and 1980s, as much as it does to the unnamed narrator of Treichel's *Der Verlorene* – his only contact with the world outside is television which he watches with both awe and feelings of shameful intimacy with his mother[18] – and Georg in *Tristanakkord*. Typically, of course, such figures never escape. Georg hence has 'Zuviel Emsfelde und zuwenig New York' (T, 190). Walser's characters, in like manner, experience the schizophrenic stresses brought about by their role-playing and longing for authenticity. His figures, furthermore, would surely empathize with Georg's botched attempts to seduce women in order to achieve some measure of *Selbstbestätigung*.

Yet there are important differences. Specifically, the significance of *Heimat* and memories of childhood diverge dramatically for the two authors. In the early Walser, and especially in *Ehen in Philippsburg* and the Kristlein trilogy, the province is regarded in an ambiguous fashion. Protagonists are embarrassed by their rustic origins and yet also inclined to locate their 'authentic selves' in their only partly repressed memories of a more innocent childhood untainted by the role-playing, crass self-exhibition and mercantile ways of the big city. In the later Walser, that is, from the mid-1970s, such ambiguity has disappeared. *Heimat* thus becomes increasingly associated with resistance to modernity, a FRG seen as technocratic and artificial rather than organic, and the dominance of an urban elite.[19] A fascination expressed in 1968 in a set of essays, *Heimatkunde* (Treichel's volume adds to this title the ironic *oder Alles ist heiter und edel*), which was conceived in part as a response to the perceived abjuration of national identity by the FRG's intellectual class, subsequently mutates into a defence of *Heimat* with a volume provocatively entitled *Heimatlob* (1978), and then finally into a celebration of the provincial and of childhood memory in *Ein Springender Brunnen* (1998). This last work exemplifies comments uttered by Walser in a discussion published in *Allemende* as recently as 1997. 'Heimat', he claims, 'ist immer das gewesen, was man nicht mehr hat'. In an era in which the 'Verlust von Heimat zugenommen und zugenommen und zugenommen [ist]', this is all the more the case. The desire is to reanimate *Heimat*, at least imaginatively.[20] *Heimat* may be something 'ungeheuer Beschränktes, etwas ungeheuer Provinzielles', but it nonetheless deserves, Walser suggests, 'das schöne Wort Kosmos. Es ist die vollkommene Geschlossenheit!'.[21] *Ein springender Brunnen* sets out to recreate this 'Kosmos', even as it risks an arguably dangerous form of historical revisionism in its detailed, almost loving depiction of its protagonist's childhood during the Third Reich.

Walser has long acknowledged the illusiveness of any Proust-like recreation of the past. An exposition of 1958, 'Leseerfahrungen mit Marcel Proust', passages in the 1964 novel *Das Einhorn*, and inserts in *Ein springender Brunnen* confirm this. Yet this does not prevent the author/narrator in the more recent novel from pursuing his 'Wunschdenkens Ziel', that is, 'ein interesseloses Interesse an der Vergangenheit'.[22] The key here is the search for genuineness in an era in which the past, so Walser argues in his controversial 1998 *Friedenspreisrede* that is often read in parallel with the novel, has been instrumentalized 'zu gegenwärtigen Zwecken'.[23] Childhood and *Heimat*, therefore, might become a repository of authenticity, if only in the imagination and by dint of repressing the depressing realization that the past can in fact never be made truly *gegenwärtig*.[24] For Walser, memories of childhood and *Heimat* are to be cleansed of Nazism so that they might offer a locus of subjective resistance to the rootlessness of the present.

Treichel also dismisses any Proustian recovery of times lost, but for different reasons. In his 2000 essay 'Lektionen der Leere. Eine Kindheit auf dem Lande. Oder wie ich Schriftsteller wurde', he suggests that the objects that he remembers from his own childhood were far less alluring than Proust's 'Madeleine-Erlebnis': 'Pappkartons', Altpapier', and 'der Geruch von Holzwolle'[25] – each of these insinuates ephemerality and intangibility. In the place of the 'fullness' conjured up by Walser, Treichel senses only emptiness: 'Die Leere ist ohne Zweifel meine prägendste Kindheitserfahrungen'. This is a metaphysical distinction. The objects that inhabit Treichel's memories possess nothing of 'vom Rilkeschen "Ding der Dinge"' nor, he asserts, anything 'vom Ding Heideggers mit seiner "verborgenen Dingheit"'. Thus there is no *presence* in Treichel's recollection of his past, no *Anwesenheit*, to use the term so beloved of conservatives when they long to invoke the past as more authentic and organic, as less complex and more immediate, something to be grasped purely sensually rather than intellectually. Treichel's past cannot be rooted in its objects; such objects provide no guarantee of authenticity nor any sense of permanence and existential security. There is nothing here of Botho Strauß' *Ästhetik der Anwesenheit*,[26] and nothing of Walser's invocation in *Ein springender Brunnen* of the redemptive 'fullness' of *Sprache* or, as he claims elsewhere, dialect.[27] Nor, for that matter, is there any hint of Arnold Stadler's invocation of a Heideggerian *Weltschmerz* that reconnects the individual alienated by modernity with the genuineness of *Heimat*, viscerality and, ultimately, death.[28] Treichel and Stadler both explore the paradoxical concept of 'Fernweh',[29] but only Stadler's figures, once abroad, yearn for that which they left behind.

Treichel's aesthetic programme is thus quite different. In *Tristanakkord*, Georg is quite simply abandoned to a present in which he is deficient and superfluous – there is no recourse to memories of a past to which he was somehow central or in which an 'authentic self' rooted in *Heimat* might be rediscovered. In his 1991 *Die Verteidigung der Kindheit*, Walser's painfully timid protagonist Alfred Dorn compensates for the supposedly American-style banality of the FRG, the Stalinistic philistinism of the GDR and the technocratic malformation, even tyranny, of both, as well as his own lack of *Anpassung* in the present-day climate of either East or West, by regathering the objects and artefacts of his Dresden childhood.[30] Treichel allows his protagonist no such comfort. Georg perceives nothing but a brutal rupture between past and present; his childhood memories, he imagines, are thus cut off from him by the river Ems, 'der Strom des Vergessens' (*T*, 17) which defines the borders of his provincial upbringing. This is his Lethe, the river at the edge of the underworld into which the dead plunge in order to forget their lives as they pass into Hades. The objects that defined the parameters of his childhood thus float away down this river of forgetting:

> Das sah er sein Leben das breite Gewässer hinabschwimmen. Sah seine Schulzeugnisse wie Laub auf dem Wasser vorbeitreiben, sah das schwarze Klavier, das leicht und wie aus Balsaholz schien, das das rostfarbene Wohnküchensofa, das samtbezogene Kissen, auf dem der Hund es sich wieder einmal unerlaubterweise bequem gemacht hatte, die Prothese seines Vaters mit dem schwarzen Lederhandschuh [. . .] und sah am Ende auch sich selbst, ungestalt und übergewichtig, mit von Frisiercreme glänzenden Haaren und einem akkurat gezogenen Scheitel, auf dem Wasser vorbei- und in Richtung Emsfelde trieben, dem nächstgelenen größeren Ort. (*T*, 18)

Noteworthy here is the passivity of the spectator, intimated by the marked absence of the pronoun and the obsessive repetition of the verb 'sah', and the wealth of outwardly realistic detail within what is obviously illusion. This is perhaps suggestive of trauma, of the hollowness of childhood memory for which these objects cannot compensate. The objects are uprooted, driven towards Emsfelde, 'dem nächstgelenen größeren Ort', and finally washed up as partial memories in Georg's present. Yet the mere fact of such 'stranded objects' from Georg's biography, to use Eric Santner's term,[31] in itself offers little prospect of redeeming either past or present. Treichel negates the potential of memory to counter the present. Thus Georg is caught in a paradoxical dialectic in which memory longs only to forget:

> Er vergaß das Klavier und die Schulzeugnisse, er vergaß den Vater und seine Prothese, er vergaß das Wohnküchensofa, den Scheitel auf seinem Schädel und das Fett in seinem Haar, das Sofa und das

Samtkissen. Nur den Hund vergaß er nicht und auch nicht, daß alles, was an ihm vorbeitrieb, Richtung Emsfelde trieb. (T, 18-19)

This dynamic defines Treichel's prose. Biography, *Heimat* and the past – none of these can offer any sense of a redemptive *Anwesenheit*. Treichel's protagonists, the nameless narrator of *Der Verlorene* as much as Georg, desire only to suppress their memories of the emptiness that infused their childhoods and of themselves either as 'ein zu dick geratener pubertierender Knabe' (V, 139) or the ungainly youth in *Tristanakkord*. This desire is reinforced by the repetition in the passage of 'er vergaß'. The objects so carefully listed are thus obsessively negated even as the urge to annul them necessarily requires Georg to recollect them in his thoughts. This process of remembering in order to forget inevitably reveals the emptiness that abides in the past. The dog, the one recollection to embody any uniqueness, 'unerlaubterweise', is the only 'object' not forgotten. This memory, however, is idiosyncratic, even comic, and not constitutive of any sense of a present self.

For Treichel, consequently, there can be no conservative fantasy of *Heimat* as a more profound reality, so to speak, that is, a reservoir of authentic feeling and experience that exposes the supposed superficiality of modern mass society with its propensity for fabricated emotion and sensationalism. Similarly, and as a result, there is no exaltation of the poetic sentimentality so often associated by Walser and others with a healthy and uninhibited national identity, and hence no recourse to a literary and philosophical tradition rooted in Romanticism that can be elevated as quintessentially German. The 'Tristanakkord', created by Wagner, perhaps the most elementally 'German' composer, would, for a Walserian character, most likely embody the traits conventionally associated with a 'German' *Weltanschauung*: 'sehnsüchtig-traurig und unerlöst' (T, 79). For Walser, as for others, a keen sensitivity towards *Weltschmerz*, sentimentality and longing defines what he sees as a positive German *Sonderweg*. A tradition of transcendent concern with *Sein* and the quest for subjective self-realization would distinguish a truly German sensibility. Much as Georg is drawn to a Wagnerian sentimentality, however, he is incapable even of recognizing the Tristan chord, despite having adopted it is as his leitmotif (T, 79).

Georg is entirely *heimatlos*. His rendition of sentimentality as an unfocused longing, rather than an attitude of revolt, is *unzeitgemäß* and unproductive. He is adrift and excess to requirements in a world geared towards achievement. The other characters in the novel, in particular Steven, an English Ph.D. student also in Bergmann's service, pursue their ambitions with far greater strategic calculation and application than Georg. They are, accordingly, scrupulously aware of their position within Bergmann's circle, business- and media-wise as regards their role in promoting their employer within the structures of the mass entertainment industry, and alive to opportunities for self-advancement. Nor can Georg's lack of contemporary adroitness be interpreted as a deliberate refusal of an inauthentic, mercantile social reality, as it might in Walser's work. His lack of rootedness in *Heimat* or memory leaves him no position from which he might criticize the present, its crude competiveness and superficiality. Andrea Köhler's suggestion of an affinity between Treichel and Walser anchored in their use of irony – she draws attention to what she calls the 'Bewusstseinsklimmzüge von Martin Walsers kartoffeltriebblassen Seelenarbeitern, denen die durchtreibende Ironie des Autors noch stets einen literarischen Heimvorteil vor den Braungebrannten und Siegesgewissen verschafft'[32] – hence requires refinement. Treichel's depiction of Bergmann and his devotees is certainly ironic, and yet Georg can gain no advantage from this satire since he has no ideals or passions, however distantly remembered, beyond the glittering world of cheap success. Instead, he is driven only by the banal ambition to emulate those around him. Appropriately enough, therefore, Georg is pathetic in the modern sense rather than in the by now almost extinguished sense of being worthy of the reader's sympathy and commitment.

In the absence of *Heimat*, there is only the seductive appeal of American-style mass culture. Despite his evident not belonging, Georg is obsessed with the icons of the culture industry. Thus he is spellbound by Bergmann, whose villas are featured in style magazines, impressed by Bergmann's assistant Bruno with his titillating insights into the private existences of his previous employers Maria Callas and Onassis, and greatly disappointed that neither Woody Allen, Madonna, Arnold Schwarzenegger nor even Paul McCartney appear as guests on the American chat show along with Bergmann: 'Er hatte sich auf Berühmtheit gefreut' (*T*, 155). In fact, he is barely able to stop himself from executing a 'Freudensprung' when invited to be present at this event (*T*, 142–3). Yet, more typically, he fails to enter into the spirit of things, a personality trait for which he blames his 'kleinliche emsländische Natur' (*T*, 126). This contradiction between unsuitability and the longing to participate in the glamour of mass culture is characteristic of Walser's figures, of course. The difference once more is that Walser's protagonists tend to possess at least a residual sense of a unique past and some recollection of personal authenticity, especially in his novels of the 1990s.[33] Georg, conversely, displays no awareness that his biography might offer any alternative, genuine counterpoint to the manufactured exuberance on a television studio tour he takes in New York: 'Die Besucher machten ebenfalls Geischter wie glückliche und erfolgreiche Menschen, nur Georg schaute sauertöpfisch drein, was ihm selbst nicht behagte, was aber wohl seine Natur war: die emsländische Natur' (*T*, 123). Nor even does the narrator appear to be willing to insinuate – perhaps against the grain of his character's thoughts – any positive value to be found in this provincial past.

Georg is, instead, humiliated by his inability to ape the spurious enthusiasm of American mass culture. Asked how he likes New York, he responds 'It's okay' in his typically impoverished English, when the required answer would have been: '"It's just great" oder "it's marvellous, it's wonderful"' (*T*, 121). Georg's replies are purely imitative and yet his mimicry is unconvincing. Despite this, he is wholly in the thrall of the clichés he has internalized from the entertainment industry. On arrival in New York, he thus perceives the city 'Wie im Film' (*T*, 101), is quite convinced his taxi driver is out to cheat him, because he has read somewhere that this is typical of New York, and is terrified of a black man with a ghettoblaster because: 'Er kannte den Typ aus dem Kino, es war der Typ Ghettohäuptling, der hochempfindlich, sehr leicht kränkbar und nachtragend ist' (*T*, 127). On no occasion is Georg able to take such clichés and undermine them in any original fashion.

Originality, of course, belongs to the Romantic concept of the artist. It might be argued, therefore, that Georg simply lacks this innovativeness and is thus unable to challenge the mundane reality in which he finds himself. Georg's artistic accomplishments are certainly slim: he has published a short volume of verse in the aptly named *Edition Ausweg*, renders poor imitations of music masters from Beethoven to Hendrix on various instruments, and copies liberally from a Georg Heym poem when asked by Bergmann to write a 'Hymne' for a new piece of music (*T*, 215-16). It is not even certain that Georg is capable of responding to art: during operas, he frequently falls asleep, a reaction he (somewhat pompously) defines as 'eine existentielle Müdigkeit' (*T*, 172) ('existentiell' is surely far too grand a term for what is most likely simply boredom!). And all this despite the fact that he claims that his model is 'Goethes junger Werther' who, so he enthuses, '[sich] dann als der größte Künstler fühlen konnte, wenn er sich in die freie Natur begab, auf einen Hügel setzte und die Sonne aufgehen ließ' (*T*, 29). Werther was in truth an artistic flop in love with a fatally idealized woman. This too Georg mimics in his adoration for Bergmann's assistant Mary, who features as his own Isolde figure in his pitiably weak echo of the Wagnerian tale of unfulfilled desire. However, at least Werther's failure – and Tristan's fate, for that matter – still have the capacity to move the audience and register some form of protest against a cruelly prosaic reality.

In fact, it is not so much originality that Georg lacks in his efforts to succeed as an artist in the age of mass culture but, once more, the capacity to forget the past and live exclusively in the moment. Bergmann, significantly, has thus managed to put his own 'emsländische Herkunft' (*T*, 23) behind him, and is, as Martin Ebel notes, 'anders als die scheiternden Helden romantischer Künstlerromane, mit seiner Kunst im Leben höchst erfolgreich'.[34] Romantic sentimentality and poignant failure are now obsolete. Presently required are self-confidence and a belief in a personal mission to succeed. Bergmann thus shows off his success with his villas and cars, throws tantrums when a piano is missing or the wrong whisky is served, and competes for media attention with his rival Nerlinger. He displays little of the metaphysical, transcendent vision of the artist. His operas tackle the big themes of life, death, sadness and happiness, but precisely in the schematic fashion implied by such a list. He thus explains to Georg that the opera *Pyriphlegethon* is about the 'Feuerstrom [. . .] der um den Tartaros fließe. In den Tartaros würden die Freveler gestoßen, die frommen Seelen dagegen gingen in die elysischen Gefilde ein' (*T*, 62). This would seem to be every bit as unoriginal as his subsequent formuliac reversal of the first piece in a follow-on work, *Elysian Fields*, which, he claims, will culminate in 'einer Art

Schlußchor, einer Apotheose auf den Frieden, das Glück, die Erlösung. Wenn auch in verrissener Zeit' (T, 148). Bergmann's claim that this would be 'völlig unzeitgemäß' (T, 148) implies less that this opera will be critical of contemporary reality than that it will fulfil the requirement that fashions should continually change. The concept 'in verrrissener Zeit' is itself, of course, a cliché, a commonplace of the contemporary sense of living in an era in which any notion of an authentic past has given way to fragmentation and arbitrary historical pastiche. Bergmann's art, indeed, has little to do with memory-work and everything to do with the commercial precepts of the culture industry. Nor does he have any real power within this system. He is dependent on the publicity generated by the talk show he 'stars' on in New York but is unable to prevent the host from trivializing his work, marginalizing his attempts at 'serious art' and controlling his exposure.

Georg is thus perhaps more insightful than he realizes when he determines that forgetting is central to the work of art in the modern era. His dissertation, he states, starts from the following premise: 'Er wollte nicht nur zeigen, daß das Geschriebene vom Autor vergessen wird. Er wollte darüber hinaus nachweisen, daß das Geschriebene nur geschrieben wird, um vom Autor vergessen zu werden' (T, 16). Memory, commonly taken to be the defining function of art, is now surplus to requirements. The present-day producer of cultural goods is no longer committed to the conservation of human experience, the recollection of utopian moments, turning points and traumas. Instead, experience is recycled and divorced from the subjective authenticity that generated it. As soon as it is reworked for mass consumption it is thus separated from the artist and quickly becomes reified as a commodity. This process denies the critical impulse that potentially inheres within memory and tends to reduce the vagaries of human experience to sensationalism.

Treichel's *Tristanakkord* is interesting insofar as it responds to the related phenomena of culture industry, Americanization and globalization in a manner that is superficially similar to writers such as Martin Walser (and perhaps Botho Strauß and Arnold Stadler) but which is in fact different in ways that define some of the faultlines in contemporary German writing. In the period since unification the conservative impulse has often been to defy what has increasingly come to be perceived as the globalization of culture and the literary marketplace by excavating 'German traditions', in particular Romanticism, and invoking *Heimat* as a locus of supposed authenticity. Ideologically and theoretically this has been underpinned by the interventions of critics such as Frank Schirrmacher and Ulrich Greiner and intellectuals such as Karl Heinz Bohrer. The appeal for a return to a more dynamic, myth-creating notion of 'memory' typically invokes Nietzsche and the idea of *In-der-Welt-Sein* and the intimate connection of Being to *Heimat* recalls Heidegger.

Treichel, on the other hand, resists the illusions of *Heimat* by refusing it any mythical quality or positive value. The same applies to memory and perhaps especially to the memory of 'German' traditions: there may be a certain nostalgia for sentimentality in the depiction of Georg but this nostalgia is not posited as a solution to the 'rootlessness' of the modern world. Yet nor does Treichel attempt to live entirely 'in the present', as many, typically younger, emergent German writers have done in the decade or so since unification. *Tristanakkord* may demonstrate a tongue-in-cheek awareness of the global vernacular of 1990s chat shows, gossip magazines, pop culture and youth fashions, as well as an occasional lightness of touch that is more usually associated with the Anglo-American narrative styles that dominate globally, yet it remains resolutely non-incorporated. For all that it rejects a conservative critique of a banal, Americanized present rooted in an appeal to German traditions and *Heimat*, it is a stubbornly modernist novel and to that extent probably acontemporary despite itself. Treichel's achievement is that he has written a text that is challenging, replete with cultural allusions and critical of present-day one-dimensionality. His novel *Tristanakkord*, in conclusion, is a complex work that challenges the contemporary globalization and homogenization of culture whilst avoiding conservative fantasies of tradition and *Heimat*.

Notes

[1] Christoph Bartmann, 'Großes Ego, kleines Ich', *Die Presse*, 25 March 2000.

[2] Ulrike Baureithel, 'Student, dem Vergessen entrissen', *Der Tagesspiegel*, 26 March 2000.
[3] Ina Hartwig, 'Die Fallhöhe der Gemeinheit', *Frankfurter Rundschau*, 4 March 2000.
[4] Martin Ebel, 'In der Komponistenumlaufbahn', *Stuttgarter Zeitung*, 21 March 2000.
[5] Tilman Krause, 'Erlöst vom Kunstwahn', *Die Welt*, 25 March 2000, 7.
[6] See my 'Hans-Ulrich Treichel's *Der Verlorene* and the "problem" of German suffering', *Modern Language Review*, January 2002.
[7] Hans-Ulrich Treichel, 'Lektionen der Leere. Eine Kindheit auf dem Lande. Oder wie ich Schriftsteller wurde', *Neue Züricher Zeitung*, 90, 15/16 April 2000, 50.
[8] Bartmann, 'Großes Ego'.
[9] Jeanette Stickler, 'Der Held fährt Trittbrett', *Rheinischer Merkur*, 25 February 2000.
[10] Michael Bauer, 'Schrille Stille', *Süddeutsche Zeitung*, 26–7 February 2000.
[11] Hartwig, 'Die Fallhöhe der Gemeinheit'.
[12] Andrea Köhler, 'Das kulturelle Gefühl', *Neue Züricher Zeitung*, 1–2 April 2000.
[13] See my *Distorted Reflections: The Public and Private Faces of the Intellectual* (Amsterdam, Rodopi, 1998) for a discussion of this tension in Walser's work of the 1960s and 1970s.
[14] Ebel, 'In der Komponistenumlaufbahn'.
[15] Hans-Ulrich Treichel, 'Prägende Sätze', *Neue Züricher Zeitung*, 235, 10 October 1998, 50. For an analysis of the theme of self-reflection in Walser's *Die Gallistl'sche Krankheit*, see my 'Martin Walser's *Die Gallistl'sche Krankheit*: self-reflexivity as illness', *German Life and Letters*, 49/3 (1996), 358–72.
[16] Köhler, 'Das kulturelle Gefühl'.
[17] Martin Walser, *Über die Schüchternheit* (Eggingen, Edition Isele, 1999), 6.
[18] *V*, 30–2.
[19] See Georg Braungart, '"Ich habe nicht das Gefühl, daß ich mich bewegt hätte." Martin Walsers "Wende" zwischen "Heimatkunde" und "Geschichtsgefühl"', in Walter Erhart and Dirk Niefanger (eds), *Zwei Wendezeiten* (Tübingen, Niemeyer, 1997), 93–114.
[20] Hermann Bauschinger, Manfred Bosch and Martin Walser (participants in a discussion), 'Heimat – aber woher nehmen?', *Allemende*, 54/55 (1997), 22–53 (26–7).
[21] Ibid., 29.
[22] Martin Walser, *Ein springender Brunnen* (Frankfurt am Main, Suhrkamp, 1998), 281.

23 Martin Walser, 'Erfahrungen beim Verfassen einer Sonntagsrede', in Frank Schirrmacher (ed.), *Die Walser-Bubis-Debatte. Eine Dokumentation* (Frankfurt am Main, Suhrkamp, 1999), 7–17 (12).

24 See my 'A manifesto for the New Right: Martin Walser, the past, transcendence, aesthetics and *Ein springender Brunnen*', *German Life and Letters*, 53/1 (2000), 126–41.

25 Treichel, 'Prägende Sätze'.

26 Botho Strauß, *Der Aufstand gegen die sekundäre Welt: Bemerkungen zu einer Ästhethik der Anwesenheit* (Munich, Hauser, 1999).

27 Hermann Bauschinger, Manfred Bosch and Martin Walser, 'Heimat — aber woher nehmen?'.

28 See, for example, Arnold Stadler, *Mein Hund, meine Sau, mein Leben* (1994), *Der Tod und ich, wir zwei* (1998), or *Ein hinreissender Schrotthändler* (1999). Walser, of course, has promoted Stadler vigorously. See, for example, 'Am schönsten ist das Trotzdemschöne', in Martin Walser, *Literatur als Weltverständnis* (Eggingen, Edition Isele, 1996), 59–77. See also my '"Nichts läßt man uns, nicht einmal den Schmerz, und eines Tages wird alles vergessen sein": the novels of Arnold Stalder from *Ich war einmal* to *Ein hinreissender Schrotthändler*', *Neophilologus*, 87 (2003), 119–32.

29 Treichel, 'Prägende Sätze'. Stadler uses the term in numerous essays and novels.

30 See Stuart Parkes, 'Looking forward to the past: identity and identification in Martin Walser's *Die Verteidigung der Kindheit*', in Arthur Williams (ed.), *The Individual, Identity and Innovation: Signals from Contemporary Literature and the New Germany* (Bern, Peter Lang, 1994), 57–74 (66). See also Heike Doane, 'The cultivation of personal and political loss: *Die Verteidigung der Kindheit*', in Frank Pillip (ed.), *New Critical Perspectives on Martin Walser* (Columbia, Camden House, 1994), 156–75.

31 Eric Santner, *Stranded Objects: Mourning, Memory and Film in Postwar Germany* (Ithaca, Cornell University Press, 1990).

32 Köhler, 'Das kulturelle Gefühl'.

33 See my 'A matter of perspective?: Martin Walser's fiction in the 1990s', in Martin Kane (ed.), *German Literature after Unification* (London, Macmillan, 2002).

34 Ebel, 'In der Komponistenumlaufbahn'.

8

'Caravaggio in Preußen': Hans-Ulrich Treichel's *Der irdische Amor*

RHYS W. WILLIAMS

The rudiments of this brilliantly comic novel are wholly familiar to Treichels's readers. We encounter a naïve, insecure, still adolescent hero, Albert, from whose perspective the narrative unfolds. Some German critics immediately spotted a connection to Goethe's *Die Leiden des jungen Werther*, in which the emotionally charged hero is contrasted with a more rational counterpoint in the figure of Albert, the husband of Lotte, who becomes the focus of Werther's passion. The resonance of names is hard to resist, but this Albert is much more like Werther himself, and the analogy beguiling but misleading. Our Albert resembles, if anything, a Kafka figure, and it is no coincidence that Kafka's *Die Verwandlung*, in a dual-language edition, is the text chosen by Albert to read with Elena to improve her German. As with Kafka's stories we are vouchsafed insights, through a third-person narrative, into the innermost thoughts of a self-doubting central character and follow him (in this case Albert) through the stages of a love affair with Elena, a young Sardinian woman. This 'hero-view' narrative is disconcerting, but is a central component of the novel, for Treichel is fundamentally less interested in the world which the hero encounters than in the comic disparities between that world and the fantasies within the central character's mind.

Thematically, the story hardly surprises those familiar with Treichel's writing. The hero is a young, intellectually ambitious student, not a young writer as in *Tristanakkord*, but an equally insecure art historian. The satirical perspectives on the German university system, in which Treichel demonstrates consummate skill and, one suspects, not a little personal animus, are transferred here from the 'Germanist' to the art historian, though the targets appear virtually identical. Treichel's criticism of what, as a creative writer, he can now afford to regard as a secondary activity, is informed by his own wide academic experience, reflected in his Ph.D. on Wolfgang Koeppen, his work on the Koeppen edition, his *Habilitationsschrift, Auslöschungsverfahren. Exemplarische Untersuchungen zur Literatur und Poetik der Moderne* (1995) and his collection of critical essays *Über die Schrift hinaus* (2000). Treichel, then, is all too familiar with the intellectual games and the posturings of academic life.

A further element which readers will find familiar is his concern with sexuality. His young heroes are sexually obsessed, insecure, voyeuristic. Their insecurity manifests itself now in assertiveness and aggression, now in embarrassment and evasion. What is common to both reactions is the overriding comic perspective from which both sides are illuminated and undermined. Treichel's heroes regard themselves as sexually maladjusted, but their obsessions emerge, through his fictions, as mildly embarrassing. The embarrassment about sexuality, which was depicted so vividly in *Der Verlorene* from the point of view of an adolescent, re-emerges here in the student Albert.

The plot of the novel is simply retold: Albert, a student of art history in Berlin, falls in love with an Italian waitress in a Berlin bar. His earlier sexual history, in boarding school and in the swimming pools of his youth, suggest a voyeuristic obsession which suddenly focuses on Elena, the Italian girl on to whom he projects an image of Italy shaped by the films of *Neoverismo* and by the radical student experience of the early 1970s. Treichel's autobiographical impetus in the *Frankfurter Poetikvorlesung* helps to explain the importance of Italy to Albert's (and Treichel's) generation. Inspired by contemporary literary antecedents, in particular Alfred Andersch's *Die Rote* and Peter Schneider's *Lenz,* Treichel signed up for Italian language courses at university and attended a seminar in the politics department on the history of the Italian Communist Party: 'Ich habe mich damals [. . .] auf durch und durch spontane und vollkommen authentische Weise nach Italien gesehnt, auch wenn ich feststellen mußte, daß sich in diesem Wintersemester, es war um 1975 herum, komplette germanistische Grundkurse nach Italien zu sehnen begannen' (*EA,* 73). Albert, no doubt conditioned by similar political and cultural values, cannot but find Elena irresistible. The reader, aware of his conditioning, is all too sceptical. This ironic distancing between the reader and

Albert, the tension between innocence and knowingness, is the prerequisite for the exquisite sense of embarrassment which pervades the text. The reality of Albert's relationship with Elena: furtive groping on a bench in the zoo in sight of the inevitably laughing hyenas, is contrasted with the idealized passion which he projects on to his pursuit of her. His linguistic shortcomings merely serve to bestow on her least remark interpretations which strike the reader as inappropriate, even incongruous. Elena, far from embodying an ideal of chaste womanhood, is quite candid about her occasional affair with a visiting Iranian businessman. Her matter-of-fact style is at odds with Albert's emotional intensity, much as her domestic arrangements fail to live up to his picturesque expectations of Italian life. Albert resolves to accompany Elena back to Sardinia, where she plans to open a beauty parlour; the disparity between their intellectual interests is throughout more apparent to the reader than to Albert. Again, Albert's expectations of continuing with his research in Sardinia are dashed by the banality of life in the industrial town of Carbonia. His encounter with the sobering ordinariness of Italian life and the fact that Elena appears far less exotic in her own surroundings prompt a trial separation which they both realize will be permanent. Albert, like the hero of Peter Schneider's *Lenz*, returns to German realities a wiser man, though we remain doubtful as to whether he will, like the central figure in a traditional *Bildungsroman*, be able to enter the adult world and function in it effectively.

The title of the novel, *Der irdische Amor*, is a reference to Caravaggio's painting of that name, a painting on which Albert is planning to write his dissertation. The choice of this particular painting is an inspired one, for it enables Treichel to explore, through Albert's research, interpretations of the picture which simultaneously highlight themes and motifs within the novel. A painting which depicts the triumph of earthly love over the arts and sciences has obvious parallels with Albert's difficulties in balancing his sexual obsessions with his academic work. The topic of homoeroticism is likewise relevant both to the painting and to various recalled episodes in Albert's earliest sexual experiences. Moreover, Albert's decision to change his dissertation topic from *Amor als Sieger* to *Der ungläubige Thomas*, suggests that his own excursion into earthly love is fast turning him into a more sceptical person. The choice of Caravaggio also underlines the link with

Albert's earlier experiences in Rome and his passion for all things Italian. But the location of the painting in the Dahlem gallery and its own history suggest that Berlin offers a significant counterpoint to the Italian experience. The fate of the Caravaggio paintings, as we shall see, comes to epitomize post-war German experience and offers a surprising parallel to Treichel's novel *Der Verlorene*. Finally, the academic apparatus and Albert's encounter with the secondary literature on Caravaggio supply some splendid opportunities for the kind of satire of the university system which is a central component of Treichel's writing.

Even before the Caravaggio painting is introduced to the reader, the context suggests that its significance for Albert is as a counter-statement to his own sexual insecurity. Arrested during a police drugs raid on their flat in Rome, Albert and his German friends are forced to sit in a police van in the company of a young policewoman who bears a resemblance (to Albert at least, who has derived his image of Italy in part from the cinema) to the young Claudia Cardinale. Albert, exposed in his pyjamas to the gaze of the policewoman, is 'der jungen Frau hoffnungslos unterlegen. Als würde er gänzlich nackt vor ihr sitzen' (*iA*, 16). Albert's involuntary sexual arousal and his profound embarrassment seem to epitomize his whole adolescent sexuality, 'die ganze Pein seiner Pubertät' (*iA*, 9), 'das ganze Unglück seiner Pubertät und Adoleszenz' (*iA*, 20). Caravaggio's painting offers Albert a radical alternative to his own adolescent experience:

> Das, was ihn an dem Knaben von Anfang an vor allem fasziniert hatte, war dessen körperlichen Unbefangenheit. Der Amor machte ihm vor, wie man sich in seiner nackten Knabenhaut auch fühlen konnte: beneidenswert unbekümmert und selbstsicher. Caravaggios Amor schien zudem beflügelt vom erwachenden Geschlechtstrieb, ohne davon geplagt zu sein. Albert dagegen hatte sich immer zernagt und angefressen gefühlt. (*iA*, 27)

Here, early in the narrative, we are given an emblematic signal of Albert's problem: his compulsive scratching, his self-mutilation, is an outward manifestation of a sense of sexual inadequacy and uncertainty, while the boy in the painting exhibits no such uncertainties.

While it is made abundantly clear that Albert is not sexually aroused by the figure of the boy in Caravaggio's painting – 'Er war nicht sonderlich an nackten Jünglingen interessiert' (iA, 26) and 'Der Amor sagte ihm als männliches Wesen nicht unbedingt zu' (iA, 27) – his reaction clearly indicates that the painting triggers a highly personal response. When he embarks on his essay plan for Professor Delbrück, Albert focuses on details in the painting which correspond to his own powerful sexual obsessions with women. His repeated visits to the gallery in Dahlem and his intensive preoccupation with the painting, coupled with his own sense of sexual need, prompt him to make what he presents as an important discovery: namely, that the fold of cloth immediately below the penis of the figure bears a resemblance to female genitalia: 'Insofern war es auch kein Problem fur ihn, sich schließlich seiner eigentlichen These zuzuwenden und mit dem Leuchtzeiger erst den herzförmigen Außenumriß der Scham, dann den scharfen Kniff und schließlich die Spiegelachse nachzuzeichnen, die er der Einfachheit halber Anus-Vulva-Achse nannte' (iA, 29). Whether Albert is projecting into the painting his own obsession, or whether he is merely reading out of the painting an implied meaning, he certainly believes that he has made a discovery. To his disappointment, Professor Delbrück not only points out that this interpretation is a commonplace among Caravaggio critics, but also seems inclined to deconstruct Albert's thesis as the product of an unhealthy obsession: 'Sie haben nicht genug Distanz zu Caravaggio' (iA, 31), is his supervisor's judgement, which is then followed up with the demeaning question as to whether Albert has a girlfriend. The first comment echoes Albert's encounter with a member of the museum staff, who calls out 'Abstand, bitte!' (iA, 32) when Albert ventures too close to the painting in the gallery; the second question is, of course, the cardinal issue around which the novel turns.

When Delbrück dismisses Albert's discovery as a commonplace, he certainly has the backing of secondary sources. Herwarth Röttgen in his book-length study *Caravaggio Der irdische Amor oder Der Sieg der fleischlichen Liebe* (1992) employs language which is distinctly similar to Albert's to describe the fold of cloth: 'Ein scharfer und an dieser Stelle eigentlich überraschender Faltenkniff, der in einer Vertiefung endet, wird von einer dreieckigen, fast herzartigen Form gerahmt, plastisch herausgehoben. Es ist die Form einer Vulva, der weiblichen Scham'.[1] This observation, which is attested as a frequently noted one, leads Röttgen to the conclusion that what is being depicted in Caravaggio's painting is an 'atto coppulativo'. Small wonder, therefore, that the painting acquires such significance for Albert. Incidentally, Albrecht Wilkens, in his 2001 Berlin dissertation 'Licht und Gewalt bei Caravaggio', makes an identical point and acknowledges in a footnote that he owes the observation to Professor Klaus Heinrich, his own supervisor, whose colloquium on Caravaggio took place in the Freie Universität Berlin in the summer term of 1987.[2] It is not too fanciful to see Albert perhaps as one of the participants in that colloquium and Klaus Heinrich as a model for Delbrück. It becomes clear, too, that Treichel is no stranger to the secondary literature on Caravaggio.

Albert's first confrontation with academic criticism, culminating in Delbrück's suggestion that he consider changing his degree subject, or at least his topic, is succeeded by a number of chapters which outline his relationship with Elena. But in Chapter Five, after a characteristic set of reminiscences about his early life, Albert's humiliation in his 'Zwischenprüfung' is described. Here he is confronted with Delbrück's assistant, who with scant disregard for the feelings of the examinee, manages both to show off his own narrow specialism and to sneer at the ignorance of his victim. All Treichel's considerable comic skills are orchestrated to perfection in this episode. The experience almost destroys Albert's interest in art history: his overriding concern was female beauty (especially that of the girls in bathing costumes whom he watched with such ingenuity through a hole bored in a newspaper). The aridity of academic specialization and its disjunction with the life needs of its young victims are evoked with splendid irony. The interest shown by art historians in the physical details of figures depicted seems to offer Albert insight into his own obsessions, but art historical debate manages, tantalizingly for him, to de-eroticize and intellectualize its subject.

One of the most amusing episodes involves just this disjunction between eroticism and academic discourse. A visiting American academic, George Robert Davidson of the University of Chicago, has announced a lecture series on 'The Naked and the Nude in Western Visual Culture', and in one particular lecture planned to speak on 'Jesus' penis, Mary's Breasts, and other nakedness in Christian Art'. Even as the lecture progresses, Albert is increasingly stimulated and distracted by the erotic presence of an attractive woman sitting next to him. While Davidson illustrates the enormous interest taken in the baby Jesus' penis by the surrounding figures in paintings by Hans Baldung Grien and Bellini, Albert gains the growing, albeit entirely misguided, impression that the woman sitting next to him is moving her thigh closer to him. As Davidson moves on to discuss paintings of Jesus as a man, covered with a cloth but showing unmistakable signs of sexual arousal beneath the cloth, Albert is moved to place his hand on her thigh. The woman screams, elbows him in the face and leaves the auditorium; all eyes turn towards him and with the intention of apologizing, he follows the woman out into the corridor and ends up incurring the wrath of the caretaker as he enters the ladies' toilet in search of the woman. She is nowhere to be seen and he is escorted out by the suspicious caretaker. As the lecture ends and the audience streams out of the lecture theatre Albert is forced to take refuge in the gentlemen's toilet. We leave him in abject misery, surrounded by the obscene graffiti on the toilet walls. The reader is drawn to concur with Delbrück that Albert should consider studying quite a different subject.

That Treichel has researched Albert's thesis topic thoroughly emerges in an episode late in the novel. Having arrived in Carbonia, Albert spends the morning reading an article on chiaroscuro in Caravaggio's painting. Even as he attempts to concentrate on his research, he is distracted by Elena's customer, who has clearly come to the beauty parlour to have unwanted hair removed. As Elena examines her, Albert is again aroused. The voyeurism which emerges throughout the novel and which is implicitly, at least, suggested by the Caravaggio painting, *Der irdische Amor*, is here most explicit. When Albert reports to Elena on his research progress, he indicates what he has been reading:

> Albert aber erzählte [. . .] von dem Aufsatz, in dem unter anderem behauptet wurde, daß es sich bei Caravaggios Helldunkel um eine Vermenschlichung der Bildfarbe insgesamt handele, da sich besagtes Helldunkel in den Grundfarben des Inkarnats manifestiere. Daß also nicht nur die Menschen bei Caravaggio nackt seien, sondern die Welt der Gegenstände überhaupt, und daß er darum zu einem sogenannten Connubium der Dinge komme. Vom bruchstückhaften Ätherblau des Himmelglobus, der hinter dem rechten Oberschenkel des *Amore vincitore* hervorschaue, einmal abgesehen. (*iA*, 200)

Treichel's source here is Andreas Prater's book *Licht und Farbe bei Caravaggio* (1992), which concludes his examination of Caravaggio's chiaroscuro with the following series of statements:

> Doch erst das tenebröse Helldunkel Caravaggios [. . .] bedeutet gleichzeitig auch eine Durchdringung der gesamten Bildwelt mit den Grundfarben des Inkarnats, [. . .] die eine 'Vermenschlichung' genannt werden könnte. Und so ist das Inkarnat [. . .] 'Anstifter' und 'Anführer' eines farbigen Connubiums der Dinge [. . .].[3] Außer dem Ätherblau des Himmelsglobus [. . .] ordnet sich alles der halb- und unbunten Chromatik des Inkarnats unter.[4]

More important than the fact of Treichel's use of secondary sources is its function. The painting and its interpretation have a double thematic function. The triumph of earthly love, the eroticism of the painting itself, acts as a cipher for Albert's own longings. His sexual insecurities are challenged by the painting; the 'amor vincit omnia' motif proves in his case to be ironically reversed. His embarrassment and furtiveness contrast with the open sexual triumphalism of the painting. But the inclusion of secondary literature on Caravaggio has the quite different function of contrasting academic writing with lived experience. Its language stands in ironic contrast to the ways in which Albert and Elena communicate. Her reaction to Albert's account of the Prater text is characteristic: 'Dann seufzte sie, sagte "Mmbeh", was eine dieser italienischen Lautfolgen war, deren Bedeutung man sogleich verstand, ohne daß man sie auch nur annähernd präzise in Worte fassen konnte' (*iA*, 201). The over-intellectualized language of Prater stands in ironic contrast to Elena's inarticulacy. Albert operates comfortably in neither sphere: he cannot intellectualize away his sexual urges and promptings, but he is intellectual enough to suffer acute embarrassment at the realities of physical sexuality.

There is a further piquancy in Albert's choice of Caravaggio. Rendered uncertain after his first meeting with Delbrück about his choice of *Amore vincitore*, he reflects on other possibilities. This moment of indecision allows Treichel a highly amusing excursus on the pedagogical problems of teaching mature students. Albert is struck by the fact that the mature students who are living on fat pensions can travel the world and see Caravaggio's works in galleries far and wide. 'Sie reisten bis nach Detroit, Kansas City and Hartford in Connecticut, was im Grunde jedes weitere Gespräch mit ihnen überflüssig machte. Wer beispielsweise Caravaggio's *Der heilige Franziskus in Exstase* im Hartforder Wodsworth Atheneum mit eigenen Augen gesehen hatte, der war für jede Seminardiskussion unbrauchbar geworden' (*iA*, 154–5).[5] Even Delbrück finds it impossible to counter the arguments of mature students who have had the advantage of seeing the original paintings and, an unwilling traveller, concentrated on the two paintings which were to be found in and around Berlin: *Amore vincitore* and *Der ungläubige Thomas*. The former was in the Dahlem Gallery, the latter in Potsdam and thus now accessible after the fall of the Berlin Wall. Berlin also possessed a copy of a Caravaggio, but three further paintings had been missing, presumed destroyed, since the end of the war. Caravaggio's work becomes, by an accident of German history, symbolic both of the destruction of Berlin in 1945 and of the subsequent division.

Treichel's interest in Caravaggio may well have been stimulated by the exhibition 'Caravaggio in Preussen. Die Sammlung Guistiniani und die Berliner Gemäldergalerie', which was first shown in the Palazzo Gustiniani in Rome and subsequently in Berlin. The exhibition, which opened in Berlin on 15 June 2001 and ran until 9 September 2001, brought together paintings which had been part of the original Guistiniani collection and explored the impact of Caravaggio on subsequent painting, particularly in Holland. The catalogue and the publicity material for the exhibition featured the most famous of the Berlin paintings, *Amore vincitore*. Moreover the exhibition served to bring together what had been a divided German collection since 1945. The Guistiniani collection, formerly owned by Vincenzo Guistiniani (1564–1637), for whom Caravaggio painted *Amore vincitore*, was purchased by the Prussian state in November 1815, a few months after the Battle of Waterloo. It became a central part of the art collection of the Altes Museum, designed by Schinkel, and opened by Frederick William III in 1830.[6] The collection was moved to the Kaiser-Friedrich Museum (now known as the Bode Museum), when it was opened in 1904. In March 1945 urgent efforts were made to bring the paintings in the galleries on the Museumsinsel to safety. Some paintings had been transported to bunkers in Friedrichshain, though the bulk of the works were driven south to be stored in mineshafts south of Eisenach. Shortly after the fall of the city Soviet troops took over the bunkers and a disastrous fire occurred, destroying many works.

Meanwhile, the pictures stored near Eisenach fell into American hands and were transported to Wiesbaden, whereupon 202 paintings were selected for transport to Washington. After the pictures had been displayed in Washington and sent on tour to other American cities, the Berlin paintings were returned to Wiesbaden in 1949. After much legal wrangling the paintings were released to Berlin in 1955 and were exhibited in the Dahlem Museum. It was from these paintings and others on loan from several European galleries that the 'Caravaggio in Preußen' exhibition was constituted. Prominent in the exhibition was a plaque which drew attention to the fact that three Caravaggios were 'vermutlich 1945 verbrannt im Flakturm Friedrichshain'.

There has been considerable speculation about the fate of these paintings, as Bodo Mrozek recently outlined in his article 'Die Akte Caravaggio'.[7] According to official reports the fires in the Friedrichshain bunker were started sometime between 5–18 May 1945 by fanatical Nazis who wished to prevent the paintings (ten by Rubens, six by van Dyck, three by Veronese, three by Caravaggio and other individual works) falling into Russian hands. Mrozek expresses some scepticism about this account, contrasting the efficiency with which the Russians guarded other valuable assets with their apparent casualness here. Moreover, he quotes Russian sources, newly available, that suggest that the paintings had already been removed from Friedrichshain to the mineshafts near Eisenach. Nor is the story correct, Mrozek asserts, that only those paintings too big for the mineshaft remained at Friedrichshain. None of the missing paintings was too large. Mrozek's suggestion is that the paintings ended up either in American private collections as personal booty, or were perhaps stolen by German soldiers on the orders of a high-ranking Nazi. In the present context it is not difficult to see the relevance of the missing Caravaggios to Treichel's personal situation. In the confusion of flight from the Red Army his own brother disappeared. In *Der Verlorene* the missing boy has a presence which is all the more powerful for his absence. It is not too fanciful to suggest that perhaps the missing Berlin Caravaggios have helped to render the surviving paintings the more significant. Perhaps, in other words, the challenge presented by the *Amore vincitore* to Albert's fragile sense of his own identity is magnified by the unconscious awareness of the absence of the three other works.

Through the choice of Caravaggio's painting as a subject for his central character's art historical research, Treichel manages to light upon a subject which can simultaneously provide a focus for Albert's psychosexual problems, offer excellent material for academic satire, and supply, through the history of the painting, a sense of both the chaotic world of Germany in 1945 and the more recent experience of unification. In his Frankfurt lectures Treichel had set out a topography of experience, concentrating above all on the 'Ostwestfalen' of his youth, the Berlin of his student years and on his beginnings as a prose writer in Rome. In a sense all three are co-present in the painting: the insecurities of his early years are suggested by the contrast with the young boy in the painting, with his sheer sexual self-confidence; Berlin is evoked through the dogged concentration of both Albert and Delbrück on the two remaining Berlin Caravaggios; and the Italian setting, in particular the Roman episode with which the novel begins and the Sardinian experience with which it concludes, are clearly central to Albert's development.

Albert is, as indicated above, a characteristic Treichel figure. The key to his insecurity lies in his childhood and in particular in his relationship with his mother. The processes of reminiscence in Treichel's works involve a painful and gradual confrontation with the deepest recesses of the self. The visit to Rome and the embarrassment of the incident with the policewoman is the first engagement with the past, but as the novel progresses, the forays into the past take us ever deeper into Albert's background and explore earlier phases of his upbringing. Chapter Three presents the adolescent years in what we know from earlier Treichel novels to be a boarding school in Hessen. Here Albert, with parents who were refugees from the eastern territories and ran first a lending library and then a wholesale meat business (both features of Treichel's own background) and Katharina, his girlfriend, seek refuge from what are characteristic West German values in the 1960s. His background is one of vulnerability and the desire for social and financial success, while she is the product of a family which has already achieved a financial stability unaffected by the war. Here two characteristic products of the post-war 'economic miracle' meet, each seeking something quite different. Katharina is seeking to shock her complacent parents through her involvement with a rebellious modern radical, complete with his volumes of Marcuse,

Kropotkin, Freud, Malinowski and Wilhelm Reich. This is the heady brew of the student revolt in the late 1960s and early 1970s, and Katharina is clearly playing with fire. Albert, by contrast, is seeking acceptance and recognition, playing out in a second generation the outsider's refugee status of his background. Katharina, if not her parents, is all too willing to accept him, though their relationship transgresses all the rules of the boarding school. Transgression is an essential component of Albert's social experience. Albert's relationship with Katharina is presented as an early rebellion against bourgeois values, those very values which her parents, with their villa in Würzburg and their holiday home in Spain, represent. The lovers' trysts take place in a copse near the school, hinting at the kind of regression to a pre-civilized existence depicted in Malinowski's seminal work *The Secret Life of Savages in North-Western Melanesia: An Ethnographical Account of Courtship, Marriage and Family Life among the Natives of the Trobriand Islands, British New Guinea* (1929), from which a quotation on infantile sexuality is included in the novel. Small wonder that an adolescent whose reading is Malinowski, Wilhelm Reich's *Die Funktion des Orgasmus*, Marcuse's *Versuch über die Befreiung* and Kropotkin's *Memoiren eines Revolutionärs* should interpret his sexual behaviour as profoundly subversive, and this is precisely how Katharina's parents view their daughter's relationship with him. The scene in which Albert visits Katharina's parents' home to request that they be allowed to see one another is a masterpiece of social embarrassment. Albert, wearing his wholly inappropriate black fur coat (which he refuses to take off), views himself as the anarchic outsider, storming the bastions of bourgeois power and privilege. But in reality he is insecure, embarrassed and ill at ease. To calm his nerves he rolls a cigarette, prompting Katharina's horrified mother to open a window and then to fetch an ashtray from another room. The humour derives from the disparity between the relatively trivial *faux pas* and the shock and horror which it provokes, between Albert's image of himself as a crusading revolutionary and the sheer respectability of the situation. To add piquancy to the whole episode, Treichel locates it as a flashback in Albert's mind even as he engages in furtive sex with Elena on the park bench watched by the barely amused hyenas.

Shame and embarrassment are part of Albert's earliest recollection, much as they characterize the upbringing of the first-person narrator in *Der Verlorene*. These emotions manifest themselves physically as a tension and itchiness which Albert seeks to relieve by scratching. Only in the swimming pool is his itchiness temporarily alleviated. But swimming pools entail confrontations with girls and he recalls as an 'Urszene' watching through a hole bored in a comic as the girl he most desires kisses a school friend and the girl responds by sticking her tongue in the boy's ear. This act of voyeurism is repeated later in Berlin as he watches a bikini-clad woman through a hole in a newspaper: 'Nur ein einziges Mal hatte er ein Loch in die Frankfurter Allgemeine Zeitung gebohrt und sich dabei genauso kümmerlich wie als pubertierender Knabe gefühlt' (*iA*, 105). The act of voyeurism triggers the memory of earlier inadequacies. Although he is eventually emboldened to approach the woman and invite her for coffee, she rebuffs him brusquely. His reaction is again characteristic: he looks again at her and finds her suddenly repulsive: 'ihr Bauchnabel ekelte ihn' (*iA*, 107). The mechanism is almost self-fulfilling: Albert projects on to the object of his desire his own fantasies and then responds with revulsion, even anger, when those fantasies fail, as they must inevitably do, to correspond with reality.

A further early memory throws light on Albert's relationship with his mother. Albert had long thought that his mother suspected that he was homosexual, largely because he never spoke about girlfriends. He in turn refused to speak about girlfriends because he did not see why he should have to prove to his mother that he was not homosexual. This particular mind game is clearly a factor in Albert's interpretation of Caravaggio's *Der irdische Amor*. But there are more serious confusions at stake: 'Sie hatte Albert gegenüber einmal zugegeben, daß er eigentlich ein Mädchen hätte werden sollen. Sie hatte sich eine Tochter gewünscht, und während ihrer Schwangerschaft sei sie auch sicher gewesen, daß er ein Mädchen sei' (*iA*, 142). While his mother insisted that she had not been disappointed when he was born, he had always remained unconvinced, for in photographs of a children's birthday party he is shown wearing girl's clothes. While it is unclear to the reader whether Albert's mother seriously dressed him as a girl out of psychological necessity or whether the explanation was more prosaic and the party simply a fancy dress party, it is evident that Albert is convinced that his mother's subsequent acts of kindness and solicitude are secret efforts to assuage her guilt, to make reparation, for this psychological crime. The relationship is symbolically re-enacted with the ritual of the ham rolls which she lovingly prepares for his journey back to Berlin and which he ritually disposes of in the litter bin. While the swimming-pool incident is presented as a possible 'Urszene', this ritual played out between mother and son perhaps offers a more convincing explanation for Albert's inability to form lasting relationships.

In a manner reminiscent of Alfred Andersch's Italian novel *Die Rote* (an influence[8] which he readily acknowledges), Treichel introduces into his text works of literature, psychology and political philosophy, in addition to the substantial art historical material. Like Andersch he is seeking to give the reader insight into the inner workings of the central character's mind, into his taste and values; at the same time the selected texts epitomize the tastes and values of a whole generation of young intellectuals in West Germany at the time. Like Andersch, he also refers to films. Two works in particular seem to have a special significance for Albert: Pier Paolo Pasolini's *Accattone* (1961) and Andrey Tarkovsky's *Stalker* (1979). Significantly, the former is alluded to during the first half of the novel, while the latter is introduced towards the end. Based on his short story 'Una vita violenta', Pasolini's film debut, *Accattone*, offers an unsentimental depiction of the bleak lives of pimps and prostitutes in the slums of Rome. The moored boat, the 'Carmelo Ciriola', which serves as a swimming pool and restaurant, is a feature of the Roman landscape which acquires special significance for Albert: 'Der Film hatte ihn überhaupt erst auf das Badeboot aufmerksam gemacht' (*iA*, 24). It is underlined here that Albert's Italian journey has been undertaken with a set of cultural preconceptions through which he sees the city. The boat appears in two scenes in the film: at the beginning, when the gang of pimps sit drinking, and later in the evening, when the character Stella is being groomed as a prostitute by Accattone. The film conjures up a conventional image of the squalor of Rome, but in depicting relationships between the sexes as exploitative and disillusioning it also prefigures Albert's unsatisfactory relationship with Elena.

Just as Albert shifts from working on Caravaggio's *Der irdische Amor* to *Der ungläubige Thomas*, so too the transition from Pasolini to Tarkovsky signals a change in his relationship to Elena. In Tarkovsky's bleak film three characters (the eponymous stalker, a science professor and a writer) enter a mysterious Zone, an area in which a meteorite is supposed to have crashed, but in which odd events seem to take place. They are seeking the Room, a place at the heart of the Zone, in which one's innermost desires will be fulfilled. The setting is a bleak and desolate industrial wasteland (not unlike the Carbonia in which Albert is living) and the journey arduous and hazardous, achievable only with the help of an experienced guide, the stalker. After lengthy debates about the arts and the sciences the characters pause on the threshold of the Room and decide to return to the normal world without having entered. Clearly, again, there are parallels with Albert's situation: he, too, opts to return to the normal world of Berlin, as if aware that life with Elena will not be an expression of his innermost wishes; he, too, is made aware that the arts and the sciences do not provide the answers to his questions. His quest for fulfilment through adopting a different Italian identity is doomed to failure. He will always remain linguistically and culturally an outsider in Sardinia. Far from enabling him to resolve his problems by stepping into an alien world, his experience with Elena simply reinforces his sense of not belonging. The chance encounter with an attractive German girl (and one from Westfalen to boot) crystallizes his decision to return to Germany. He will, the reader presumes, still have his difficulties with the opposite sex, but at least a whole set of cultural and linguistic problems will be obviated.

In a recent review of Treichel's three novels Gerhard Henschel notes that despite his efforts to distance himself from his narrators, Treichel finds it difficult to dissipate the impression that he is drawing on his personal life for his fiction. Enough of these academic and social failures from Westfalen, Henschel cries: 'Jetzt würde es den treuen Leser der autobiographisch gefärbten Romane von Hans-Ulrich Treichel interessieren, wie der nächste Held mit dem Glück und dem Erfolg zurechtkommt'.[9] There are, of course, similarities between Treichel's central characters, though the shift from first-person narrator in *Der Verlorene* to the third-person in *Tristanakkord* and *Der irdische Amor* should not be overlooked. Yet if Henschel is seeking confident, well-adjusted narrators he will also have to forfeit precisely those qualities which are the hallmarks of Treichel's writing. It is the insecurity of his central characters which makes them perfect vehicles for Treichel's comic vision. Classical comedy traditionally dealt in aberrations from the social norm and we were invited to laugh from a secure position within that norm *at* those who failed to conform. But in the post-Nietzschean absence of a social norm, in a world in which social conformism is itself suspect, we are more frequently invited to laugh *with* the nonconformist central character at social convention. Treichel's modern comedy hovers uneasily between these positions. His maladjusted central characters, insecure and aggressive by turn, are ideally suited to expose social conformism, in the shape of academic convention or social rigidity. We laugh *with* his central characters at the minor functionaries of a conventional society, the door-keepers, the swimming-pool attendants, the museum staff, even the academics. We are invited to share the outsider's view of social cliché and convention. At the same time, we are aware that his central characters are at odds with themselves and Treichel's irony gives us a vantage point to laugh *at* the comic disparity between Albert's fantasies and the mundane realities which act as a corrective to his expectations. The 'hero-view' narrative presents events from Albert's perspective, helping us to laugh with him, but the ironic tone allows us a vantage point outside Albert, on the side of mundane reality, as it were, from which we can view his actions and reactions as ludicrously inappropriate. It is precisely this tension which is the hallmark of Treichel's comic vision. Confident and assertive central characters comfortable with their success (as proposed by Gerhard Henschel) would remove that tension and deprive us of a whole set of comic possibilities, and contemporary German writing would be the poorer for it.

Notes

[1] Herwarth Röttgen, *Caravaggio Der irdische Amor oder Der Sieg der fleischlichen Liebe* (Frankfurt am Main, Fischer, 1992), 41.

[2] Albrecht Wilkens, 'Licht und Gewalt bei Caravaggio. Studien zur Entstehung und Wirkungs-geschichte einer epiphanen Neuerung'. The thesis was examined on 18 June 1999 and became available on 9 May 2001. See http://darwin.inf.fu-berlin.de/2001/32/ (accessed 23 August 2002).

[3] Andreas Prater, *Licht und Farbe bei Caravaggio. Studien zur Ästhetik und Ikonographie des Helldunkels* (Stuttgart, Franz Steiner, 1992), 156.

⁴ Ibid., 153.
⁵ The spelling 'Wodsworth' should be 'Wadsworth'.
⁶ I am indebted here to Rüdiger Klessmann, *The Berlin Gallery* (London, Thames and Hudson, 1971), 31–78.
⁷ 'Die Akte Caravaggio', *Frankfurter Allgemeine Zeitung*, 27 Juli 2001. The article is reproduced in full at www.satt.org/kunst/01/09/caravaggio/1.html (accessed 23 August 2002).
⁸ See *EA*, 72.
⁹ Gerhard Henschel, 'Emsfelde regiert. Der Erzähler Hans-Ulrich Treichel', *Merkur*, 57 (2003), 344–8 (here 348).

Bibliography

DAVID BASKER

CONTENTS

1. Creative writing
1.a Prose works
1.b Anthologies of poems
1.c Libretti
1.d Prose extracts and poems in anthologies and journals
1.e Newspaper publications
1.f Interviews

2. Literary Criticism
2.a Books
2.b Articles and essays
2.c Radio features
2.d Edited volumes
2.e Reviews

Works are listed chronologically.

3. Secondary Literature

Books and articles are listed alphabetically, by author's surname.

1. Creative Writing

1.a Prose works

1. *Von Leib und Seele*. Berichte (Frankfurt am Main, Suhrkamp, 1992) [paperback edition: Frankfurt am Main, Suhrkamp, 1998 [st 2924]].
2. *Heimatkunde oder Alles ist heiter und edel*. Besichtigungen (Frankfurt am Main, Suhrkamp, 1996) [paperback edition: Frankfurt am Main, Suhrkamp, 2000 [st 3111]].
3. *Der Verlorene*. Erzählung (Frankfurt am Main, Suhrkamp, 1998) [paperback edition: Frankfurt am Main, Suhrkamp, 1999 [st 3061]].
4. *Der Entwurf des Autors*. Frankfurter Poetikvorlesungen (Frankfurt am Main, Suhrkamp, 2000) [es 2193].
5. *Tristanakkord*. Roman (Frankfurt am Main, Suhrkamp, 2000) [paperback edition: Frankfurt am Main, Suhrkamp, 2001 [st 3303]].
6. *Über die Schrift hinaus*. Essays zur Literatur (Frankfurt am Main, Suhrkamp, 2000) [es 2144].
7. *Der irdische Amor* (Frankfurt am Main, Suhrkamp, 2002).

1.b Anthologies of poems

1. *Ein Restposten Zukunft*. Gedichte (Berlin, Edition Neue Wege, 1979).
2. *Tarantella*. Gedichte (Berlin, Harald Schmid, 1982).
3. *Aus der Zeit des Schweigens. Neun Lieder für Arthur Rimbaud. Ein Oratorium* (Berlin, Edition Dieter Wagner, 1984)
4. *Liebe Not*. Gedichte (Frankfurt am Main, Suhrkamp, 1986) [es 1373].
5. *Seit Tagen kein Wunder*. Gedichte (Frankfurt am Main, Suhrkamp, 1990) [es 1610].
6. *Der einzige Gast*. Gedichte (Frankfurt am Main, Suhrkamp, 1994) [es 1904].
7. *Gespräch unter Bäumen*. Gedichte (Frankfurt am Main, Suhrkamp, 2002) [st 3400].

1.c Libretti

1. *Das Badener Lehrstück vom Einverständnis,* adapted from Bertolt Brecht, with music by Paul Hindemith, first performed Märzzuschlag (Austria), 25 October 1983.
2. *Atta Troll. Ein Sommernachtstraum,* adapted from Heinrich Heine, with music by David Graham, Düsseldorf, 1984.
3. *Tre Opere per Burratini*, with music by Hans Werner Henze, first performed Montepulciano (Italy), 16 June 1984. [New arrangement by Jörg Widmann as *Knastgesänge. Drei Musiktheaterstücke für Puppenspieler, Sänger und Instrumentalisten. Variationen über vier Lieder von Hans Werner Henze (1984)*, first performed Basel, 23 March 1996.]
4. *Das Mädchen und das Ungeheuer. Szenen aus der Märchenwerkstatt. Promenadenkonzert für Sänger, Schauspieler und Instrumentalisten*, with

music by Max Koch, Olga Neuwirth, Viktor Rieá, Arno Steinwider and Hans Werner Henze, first performed Deutschlandsberg (Austria), 4 October 1986.
5. *Der Hofmeister*, adapted from Jakob Michael Reinhold Lenz, with music by Michel Reverdy, first performed Munich, 14 May 1990.
6. *Das verratene Meer. Musikdrama in zwei Akten*, adapted from Yukio Mishima, *gogo no eiko* [*Der Seemann, der die See verriet*], with music by Hans Werner Henze, first performed Berlin, 5 May 1990.
7. *Venus und Adonis. Oper in einem Akt für Sänger und Tänzer*, with music by Hans Werner Henze, first performed Munich, 11 January 1997.
8. *Sinfonia N. 9 für gemischten Chor und Orchester*, adpated from Anna Seghers, *Das siebte Kreuz*, with music by Hans Werner Henze, first performed Berlin, 11 September 1997.

1.d Prose extracts and poems in anthologies and journals
1. 'Wem gehört die Stadt', in Peter Gerlinghoff, Günter Maschuff, Hans-Ulrich Treichel (eds), *Stadtansichten. Gedichte Westberliner Autoren* (Berlin, Herrmann, 1977), 9.
2. 'Alte Tradition', ibid., 29.
3. 'Ein Brief vom Bezirksamt', ibid., 64.
4. 'Midlife', ibid., 108.
5. 'Berliner Perspektiven', ibid., 108.
6. 'Das Geschäft mit der Dialektik', ibid., 171.
7. *Nicht ewig auch unbelehrbar. Aus Anlaß der Ausstellung im Haus der Kirche, Berlin, vom 6. April – 12. Mai 1978 und der Ausstellung in der Galerie Orangerie, Köln, vom 27. Oktober – 30. November 1978. Gedichte von Hans-Ulrich Treichel* (Berlin, Edition Neue Wege, 1978).
8. 'Warum diese Angst', in Jens Brockmeier (ed.), *Orpheus Materialien* (Stuttgart, Generalintendanz der Württembergischen Staatsteater Stuttgart, 1979), 98–101.
9. 'Ich, das Erdentier', in Christoph Buchwald and Christoph Meckel (eds), *Claassen Jahrbuch der Lyrik 2. Das zahnlos geschlagene Wort* (Düsseldorf, Claassen, 1980), 29–30.
10. 'Biographie', in Ronald Glomb and Lothar Reese (eds), *Anders als die Blumenkinder. Gedichte der Jugend aus der 70er Jahren* (Reinbek bei Hamburg, Rowohlt, 1980), 37.
11. 'Sommersontag', ibid., 93.
12. 'Später Besuch', ibid., 131.
13. 'Utopische Anfrage', ibid., 132.
14. 'unemanzipiert', ibid., 132.
15. 'Gegenrede', ibid., 140.
16. 'Gegen Grenzen. Gedichte', in *Stadtansichten 1980. Jahrbuch für Literatur und kulturelles Leben in Berlin (West)* (Berlin, Herrmann, 1980), 71–3.

17. 'Vom Einverständnis', in *Park. Zeitschrift für neue Literatur*, 10 (March 1980), 18.
18. 'Sonntagnachmittag', ibid., 19.
19. 'Majakowski', in *Stadtansichten 1981. Jahrbuch für Literatur und kulturelles Leben in Berlin (West)* (Berlin, Herrmann, 1981), 14.
20. 'Rimbaud', ibid.
21. 'Dieses Land', in *Schreiben wie wir leben wollen. Ein Almanach* (Berlin, Neue Gesellschaft für Literatur, 1981), 28.
22. 'Zustände', *Omnibus*, 4 (1981), 65.
23. 'Hausordnung', ibid.
24. 'Die Bars', ibid.
25. 'Friedenszeiten', in *Berlin-Zulage. Gedichte aus der Provinz* (Berlin, Arbeitsgruppe Lyrik, 1982), 7.
26. 'Schlaflos', ibid.
27. 'Realistisch schreiben', ibid., 8.
28. 'Zustände', *Kürbiskern*, 1 (1982), 56.
29. 'Ikarus', ibid.
30. 'An uns', ibid.
31. 'Die Sirenen keuchen', in Ronald Glomb, Wolfgang Heyder, Wolfgang Kolling and Lothar Reese (eds), *Härter als der Rest. Jahrbuch für junge Lyrik* (Berlin, Oberbaum, 1983), 72.
32. 'Die Bars', ibid., 73.
33. 'In den Bruchwiesen', ibid., 74.
34. 'Wem gehört die Stadt?', in Karl Riha (ed.), *Stadtleben. Ein Lesebuch* (Darmstadt and Neuwied, Luchterhand, 1983), 22–6.
35. 'Wenn ich noch einmal in den Stadtpark dürfte', in Hans Kruppa (ed.), *Wo liegt euer Lächeln begraben? Gedichte gegen den Frust* (Frankfurt am Main, Fischer-Taschenbuch, 1983), 134.
36. 'Verführungen', in Helmut Lamprecht (ed.), *Wenn das Eis geht. Temperamente und Positionen. Ein Lesebuch zeitgenössischer Lyrik* (Fischerhude, Atelier im Bauernhaus, 1983), 106.
37. 'Hier bin ich', ibid.
38. 'Alter Bahnhof', ibid., 107.
39. 'Alter Bahnhof', in Michael Kellner and Lothar Reese (eds), *39-347: Texte von Fernweh und Reisefieber* (Reinbek bei Hamburg, Rowohlt, 1983), 53.
40. 'Über den Alpen', ibid., 110.
41. 'Toter Mann', in Rudie Finkler and Nikolaus Hansen (eds), *Unbändig Männlich. Ein Lesebuch für halbstarke Väter und Söhne* (Reinbek bei Hamburg, Rowohlt, 1983), 169.
42. 'Parsifal reitet', in Ronald Glomb and Lothar Reese (eds), *Benzin im Blut. Großstadt Lesebuch* (Reinbek bei Hamburg, Rowohlt, 1984), 101.
43. 'Grenzübergang', in Christoph Buchwald and Gregor Laschen (eds), *Luchterhand Jahrbuch der Lyrik 1984* (Darmstadt, Luchterhand, 1984), 35.

44. 'In diesen Mörderzeiten', in Manfred Hausin (ed.), *Wir haben lang genug geliebt, und wollen endlich hassen! Gedichte* (Frankfurt am Main, Fischer-Taschenbuch, 1984), 127.
45. 'Westfälische Himmelfahrt' in Ronald Glomb, Wolfgang Heyder and Lothar Reese (eds), *Geschlitztes Ohr im Himmel. Jahrbuch für junge Lyrik 1984* (Berlin, Oberbaum, 1984), 78.
46. 'Vom Wetter', ibid., 79.
47. 'Nichts wie hinaus', ibid., 107.
48. 'Das gute Gedicht', ibid.
49. 'Landschaft', in *Musikhochschule Köln Journal*, 3/2, (1984–5), 2.
50. 'Der Wind war nichts', ibid., 3.
51. 'Das Blau des Himmels', ibid., 4.
52. 'Ohne den Tag will ich leben', ibid., 5.
53. 'Seht mein Grab', ibid., 6.
54. 'Orpheus, mein glücklicher Bruder', ibid., 7.
55. 'Vergebt mir ihr Engel', ibid., 8.
56. 'ich werde allein sein', ibid., 9.
57. 'So komme ich zurück', ibid., 10.
58. 'Alter Bahnhof', in Gerald Sammet (ed.), *Gleisweise. Texte aus Zügen* (Reinbek bei Hamburg, Rowohlt, 1985), 192.
59. 'Gedichte' ['Nichts wie hinaus', 'Vom Wetter', 'So viel Vergessen', 'Herbstland', 'Parsifal reitet', 'In diesen Mörderzeiten', 'Letzte Rettung', 'Im Herbst', 'Grenzübergang', 'Novemberliebe', 'Ins Laub', 'Viel Glück'], in Fritz Deppert, Hanne F. Juritz and Karl Krolow (eds), *Literarischer März 4. Lyrik unserer Zeit* (Munich, List, 1985), 118–29.
60. 'Im Herbst', in Roland Glomb, Wolfgang Heyder and Lothar Reese (eds), *Gesang auf mein Messer. Jahrbuch für junge Lyrik 3* (Berlin, Mariannenpresse, 1985), 77.
61 'Rückwärts', ibid., 77–8.
62. 'So viel Vergessen', ibid., 78.
63. 'Curriculum Vitae', ibid., 79.
64. 'Novemberliebe', in *Berliner Autoren-Stadtbuch. 111 von A bis Z* (Berlin, Abteilung Literatur der Akademie der Künste, 1985), 200.
65. 'Woyzecks Bericht', ibid.
66. 'Im Herbst', ibid.
67. 'Fotoalbum', in Christoph Buchwald and Elke Erb (eds), *Luchterhand Jahrbuch der Lyrik 1986* (Darmstadt, Luchterhand, 1986), 37.
68. 'Sisyphos' Dementi', in *Welt der Mythen. Texte und Bilder zu den Frankfurter Festen 1987* (Frankfurt am Main, Alte Oper Frankfurt, 1987), 49.
69. 'Prometheus', ibid., 50.
70. 'Der Apokalyptische Reiter', ibid., 51.
71. 'Blätter', ibid., 52.
72. 'Mythos Berlin 1987', ibid., 53.

73. 'Wenn ich hinginge', in Michael Braun and Hans Thill (eds), *Punktzeit. Deutschsprachige Lyrik der achtziger Jahre* (Heidelberg, Das Wunderhorn, 1987), 49.
74. 'Parsifal reitet', ibid., 111.
75. 'Berliner Perspektiven', in Jutta Rosenkranz (ed.), *Berlin im Gedicht. Gedichte aus 200 Jahren* (Husum, Husum-Druck-und-Verlag-Gesellschaft, 1987), 38.
76. 'Grenzübergang', in Hans Bender (ed.), *Was sind das für Zeiten. Deutschsprachige Gedichte der achtziger Jahre* (Munich and Vienna, Hanser, 1988), 209.
77. 'Viel Glück', ibid.
78. 'Alptraum', in Hans Ulrich Hirschfelder and Gerd Nieke (eds), *Nachtstücke. Ein Lesebuch* (Frankfurt am Main, Suhrkamp, 1988), 87.
79. 'Notturno für Eurydike', ibid., 88.
80. 'Potsdamer Straße', in Urs Jaeggi (ed.), *Mauersprünge. Besondere Berliner Verkehrsformen* (Reinbek bei Hamburg, Rowohlt, 1988), 102.
81. 'Grenzübergang', ibid., 115.
82. 'Wintersonntag in Pisa', in *Italien-Dichtung Band 2. Gedichte von der Klassik bis zur Gegenwart* (Stuttgart, Reclam, 1988), 454.
83. 'Benn', in Ulrich Janetzki and Lutz Zimmermann (eds), *Anfang sein für einen neuen Tanz kann jeder Schritt. Junge Berliner Literatur der achtziger Jahre* (Berlin, Literarisches Colloquium, 1988), 149.
84. 'Blätter', ibid., 150.
85. 'Abgesang', ibid., 151.
86. 'Zum halben Preis', ibid., 152.
87. 'Halbes Libeslied für Berlin', ibid., 153.
88. 'Alles vergeht', ibid., 154.
89. 'Woyzeck', in Jan Christoph Hauschild (ed.), *Oder Büchner. Eine Anthologie* (Darmstadt, Georg-Büchner-Buchhandlung, 1988), 74.
90. 'Woyzecks Bericht', ibid., 74–5.
91. 'Woyzecks Nachtlied', ibid., 75.
92. 'Halbes Libeslied für Berlin', in *Berlin Literarisch. 120 Autoren aus Ost und West. Fotografiert und zusammengestellt von Renate von Mangoldt* (Berlin, Argon, 1988), 218.
93. 'Die Bars', in Ludwig Moos (ed.), *In Italien. Eindrücke vom Stiefel* (Reinbek bei Hamburg, Rowohlt, 1984), 154; also in Alice Frank and Christoph Klimke (eds), *Ciao Italien. Ein Land auf den zweiten Blick* (Reinbek bei Hamburg, Rowohlt, 1988), 107.
94. 'Wintersonntag in Pisa', in Günter E. Grimm (ed.), *Italien-Dichtung. Band 2. Gedichte von der Klassik bis zur Gegenwart* (Stuttgart, Reclam, 1988), 454.
95. 'Wiepersdorf, die Arnimschen Gräber', in Helmut Henne and Birgit Richter (eds), *Der unbekannte Grimm. Ferdinand und seine Brüder. Erinnerungsblätter* (Braunschweig, Meyer, 1988), 25.

96. 'Gedichte' ['Sguardo' [= 'Einscht'], 'Quello che so degli alberi' [= 'Was weiß ich von Bäumen'], 'Il Mio ordine' [= 'Meine Ordnung'], 'Per Roma' [= 'Römischer Lobgesang'], 'Notte d'estate' [= 'Sommernacht'], 'Alba' [= 'Morgenliebe']], translated by Vanda Peretta, *Jahresdokumentation. Deutsche Akademie Villa Massimo Rom* (1988-9).
97. 'Romanzero', in *Lyrik seit 1960. Poezie sinds 1960. Westfalen/Westflandern. Eine zweisprachige Anthologie* (Münster, 1989), 132.
98. 'Die Überfahrt', ibid., 133.
99. 'Über den Sonetteschreiber Brecht', ibid., 134-5.
100. 'Römischer Lobgesang', *Sprache im technischen Zeitalter*, 111 (1989), 73.
101. 'Sommernacht', ibid.
102. 'D, j. . . vu', ibid.
103. 'In den Bruchwiesen', in Ronald Glomb (ed.), *Neue deutsche Lyrik* (Munich, Heyne, 1989), 64.
104. 'Nichts wie hinaus', ibid., 65.
105. 'Westfälische Himmelfahrt', ibid., 66.
106. 'Alles vergeht', *Freitag*, 21 December 1990.
107. 'Einsicht', ibid.
108. 'Der Lyrikerpreis', ibid.
109. 'Variationen über Kain', in Dieter Rexroth (ed.), *Mensch und Mensch. Texte und Bilder zu den Frankfurter Festen 1989* (Frankfurt am Main, Alte Oper Frankfurt, 1989), 119-24.
110. 'Am Brandenburger Tor', *Dass ein gutes Deutschland blühe. Jahresgabe 1991 der Hoesch AG Dortmund* (Dortmund, Hoesch, 1991), 265.
111. 'Selbstporträt, korrigiert', in Theo Elm (ed.), *Kristallisationen. Deutsche Gedichte der achtziger Jahre* (Stuttgart, Reclam, 1992), 53.
112. 'Kleistkongreß', ibid.
113. 'Rückwärts', ibid., 54.
114. 'Gespräch unter Bäumen', in Rudolf Helmut Reschke (ed.), *Deutsche Lyrik unseres Jahrhunderts. Eine Anthologie* (Gütersloh, Bertelsmann-Club, 1992), 586.
115. 'Befund', ibid., 586-7.
116. 'Drei Lieder über den Schnee', ibid., 587.
117. 'Bahnhof Lichtenberg', *Neue Rundschau*, 103/2 (1992), 109.
118. 'Rechereche', ibid.
119. 'Politik der Lebensstile', ibid., 110.
120. 'Erste Amtshandlung', ibid.
121. 'Als ich in Rom war', *Park. Zeitschrift für neue Literatur*, 16/43-4 (1992), 8.
122. 'Im Dornbusch', ibid.
123. 'Kein Herbstgedicht', ibid.
124. 'Klassische Moderne', *Merkur* 515/2 (February 1992), 165-70.

125. 'Spätes Bildnis der Droste', in Lieselotte Folkerts (ed.), *Liebe Stadt im Lindenkranze. Münster and das Münsterland in Gedichten und Bildern. Eine Anthologie durch acht Jahrhunderte* (Emsdetten, Lechte, 1993), 177.
126. 'Eine Reise nach Stendal', *Merkur*, 531/6 (June 1993), 550–2.
127. 'Jakob van Hoddis', in Lothar Jordan and Winfried Woesler (eds), *Lyrikertreffen Münster. Gedichte und Aufsätze. 1987–91* (Bielefeld, Aisthesis, 1993), 212.
128. 'Nachtrag', ibid.
129. 'Belcanto', ibid., 213.
130. 'Politik der Lebensstile', ibid.
131. 'Erste Amtshandlung', ibid., 214.
132. 'Gregor Samsa', ibid.
133. 'Stoßgebet', ibid.
134. 'Erster Frühlingstag', *Stint. Zeitschrift für Literatur*, 7/13 (May 1993), 130.
135. 'Als ich in Rom war', ibid., 131.
136. 'Bocca della Verit...', ibid.
137. 'Im Dornbusch', ibid., 132.
138. 'Recherchen', ibid.
139. 'Londoner Auskunft', ibid., 133.
140. 'Grand Hotel Berlin Mitte', in Karl Otto Conrady (ed.), *Von einem Land und vom andern. Gedichte zur deutschen Wende* (Frankfurt am Main, Suhrkamp, 1993), 123.
141. 'Wendezeit', ibid., 125.
142. 'Der Hypochonder', in Hannes Hauser and Siegbert Metelko (eds), *Klagenfurter Texte. Ingeborg-Bachmann-Wettbewerb 1993* (Munich, List, 1993), 125–33.
143. 'Neue Gedichte' ['Stilleben', 'Stendal', 'Fragment, philosophisch', 'Erster Frühlingstag', 'Klagenfurt', 'Wendezeit', 'Nach Magdeburg'], *Neue deutsche Literatur*, 2 (94), 95–8.
144. 'Dankrede zum Förderpreis des Bremer Literaturpreises 1993', in *Verleihung des Bremer Literaturpreises 1993. Laudationes und Reden* (Bremen, Rudolf-Alexander-Schröder-Stiftung, 1994), 29–31; reprinted as 'Leerstellen meiner Biographie', in Wolfgang Emmerich (ed.), *Der Bremer Literaturpreis. Eine Dokumentation 1954–98. Reden der Preisträger und andere Texte* (Bremerhaven, Wirtschaftsverlag NW, 1999), 446–7.
145. 'Amrumer Massagen', *Freitag*, 1 April 1994.
146. 'Auf der Suche nach Venedig', *Wochenpost*, 25 August 1994.
147. 'Was der Vater sagte', *Sprache im technischen Zeitalter*, 131 (September 1994), 265–71.
148. 'Am großen Wannsee', *Merkur*, 548/11 (November 1994), 1030–3.
149. 'Hotel Salerno', in Jens Johler (ed.), *Das minimale Mißgeschick. Schadenfrohe Geschichten* (Cologne, Kiepenheuer & Witsch, 1995), 203–8.

150. 'Mortimer! Mortimer! Der Hundestrand am Berliner Grunewaldsee', *Wochenpost*, 26 January 1995.
151. 'Die Chefs der Gärtner und die Chefs der Küche. Cluburlaub in Pamphylien', *Freitag*, 21 April 1995.
152. 'Anflug Kiew', *Das Gedicht*, 3 (October 1995), 90.
153. 'Prenzlauer Bergbesteigung', ibid.
154. 'Der Negerpastor', *Merkur*, 561/12, 1156–61.
155. 'Spätes Bildnis der Droste', in Liselotte Folkerts (ed.), *Annette von Droste-Hülshoff zum 200. Geburtstag. Katalog zur Ausstellung* (Münster, L. Folkerts, 1996), 206.
156. 'Mythos Berlin', in Bernd Seidensticker and Peter Habermehl (eds), *Unterm Sternbild des Hercules. Antikes in der Lyrik der Gegenwart* (Frankfurt am Main and Leipzig, Insel, 1996), 82.
157. 'Orpheus' Abgesang', ibid., 84.
158. 'Sisyphos' Dementi', ibid., 90.
159. 'Der Schweinekopf', in Heinz-Ludwig Arnold and Christiane Freudenstein (eds), *Das literarische Bankett* (Leipzig, Kiepenheuer, 1996), 210–3.
160. 'Am Hundestrand', in Karin Kiwus (ed.), *Berlin – Ein Ort zum Schreiben. 347 Autoren von A bis Z* (Berlin, Akademie der Künste, 1996), 503.
161. 'Poetisches Portugal', *Neue deutsche Literatur*, 96/2 (1996), 85–94.
162. 'Text [1. Die Flucht, 2. Bei den Toten, 3. Bericht der Verfolger, 4. Die Platane Spricht, 5. Der Sturz, 6. Die Nacht im Dom, 7. Die Rettung] zu Hans Werner Henze: Sinfonia No. 9 und Notiz zum Text', in *Hans Werner Henze. Sinfonia No. 9. Uraufführung. Programmheft. 47. Berliner Festwochen 1997*. Reprinted in *Argonautenschiff. Jahrbuch der Anna Seghers Gesellschaft*, 7 (1998), 15–21.
163. 'Seit ich hier bin', in Christoph Buchwald and Ror Wolf (eds), *Jahrbuch der Lyrik 97–8* (Munich, Beck, 1997), 107.
164. 'Woyzeck', *Stint. Zeitschrift für Literatur*, 22/11 (November 1997), 24.
165. 'Umland', in Michael Speier (ed.), *Berlin, mit deinen frechen Feuern. 100 Berlin-Gedichte* (Stuttgart, Reclam, 1997), 106.
166. 'Ganz Berlin war mein Zimmer', in Jörg Plath (ed.), *Mein Berliner Zimmer. 25 Bekenntnisse zu dieser Stadt* (Berlin, Nicolai, 1997), 90–7.
167. 'Adonis', in Hans Werner Henze, *Venus und Adonis. Programmheft der Bayerischen Staatsoper* (Munich, Bayerische Staatsoper, 1997), 25.
168. 'Drei Lieder über den Schnee', ibid., 26.
169. 'Der Lieblingsberliner', in Sven Arnold and Ulrich Janetzki (eds), *Berlin zum Beispiel. Geschichten aus der Stadt* (Munich, Goldmann, 1997), 120–33.
170. 'Solo für die Luftgitarre', *Merkur*, 591 (June 1998), 554–60.
171. 'Letzte Rettung', in Harald Hartung (ed.), *Jahrhundertgedächtnis. Deutsche Lyrik im 20. Jahrhundert* (Stuttgart, Reclam, 1998), 298.

172. 'Der Verlorene', in Georg Bühren, Walter Gödden and Jürgen P. Wallmann (eds), *Nach dem Frieden. Anthologie* (Münster, Ardey, 1998), 112–24.
173. 'Auf der Couch', in Wolfgang Schneider (ed.), *Männerbilder. Ein Lesebuch* (Frankfurt am Main, Suhrkamp, 1998), 62–9.
174. 'Venedig', in Rainer Weiss (ed.), *Lektüre zwischen den Jahren. Träume sind wahr* (Frankfurt am Main, Suhrkamp, 1998), 60–3.
175. 'Plagwitz', in Christoph Buchwald and Raoul Schrott (eds), *Jahrbuch der Lyrik 2000* (Munich, Beck, 1999), 48.
176. 'Biographie', ibid., 49.
177. 'Interregio Berlin-Leipzig', in Dirk Dasenbrock and Marco Sagurna (eds), *Eiswasser. Echte Blüten. Neue deutsche Naturlyrik*, 5 I/II (1998), 119.
178. 'Südraum Leipzig', ibid., 120.
179. 'Platz in Wilmersdorf', ibid., 121.
180. 'In Weimar im Winter', ibid., 122.
181. 'Teiresias', ibid., 123.
182. 'Gleich hinter Torgau kreisen die Adler. Gedichte' ['Heißer Sommer', 'In Weimar im Winter', 'Interregio Berlin-Leipzig', 'Abend in Plau am See'], *Sprache im technischen Zeitalter*, 151 (October 1999), 365–6.
183. 'Mythos Berlin 1987', in Waltraud Wende (ed.), *Großstadtlyrik* (Stuttgart, Reclam, 1999), 330.
184. 'Mythos Berlin 1987', in Heinz-Ludwig Arnold (ed.), *Die deutsche Literatur seit 1945. Augenblicke des Glücks 1990–95* (Munich, dtv, 1999), 17.
185. 'Am Brandenburger Tor', ibid.
186. 'Mauergedicht', ibid., 18.
187. 'Moderne Zeiten', ibid., 332.
188. 'Wendezeit', ibid.
189. 'Hans-Ulrich Treichel über Hans-Ulrich Treichel. In sechs Stichwörtern', in Alessandra Sorbello Staub (ed.), *Hans-Ulrich Treichel. Begleitheft zur Ausstellung der Stadt- und Universitätsbibliothek Frankfurt am Main 12. Januar – 29. Februar 2000* (Frankfurt am Main, Stadt- und Universitätsbibliothek Frankfurt am Main, 2000), 9–14.
190. 'Rückfall', in Theo Elm (ed.), *Lyrik der neunziger Jahre* (Stuttgart, Reclam, 2000), 94.
191. 'Wendezeit', ibid.
192. 'Grand Hotel, Berlin Mitte', ibid., 95.
193. 'Moderne Zeiten', ibid.
194. 'Im Schwimmbad', in Christoph Buchwald and Ludwig Harig (eds), *Jahrbuch der Lyrik 2001* (Munich, Beck, 2000), 120.
195. 'Heißer Sommer', ibid., 121.
196. 'Der Verlorene', in Heinz-Ludwig Arnold (ed.), *Deutsche Literatur seit 1945. Flatterzungen 1996–9* (Munich, dtv, 2000), 250–4.

Bibliography 121

197. 'Stoßgebet', in Christoph Buchwald and Adolf Endler (eds), *Jahrbuch der Lyrik 2002* (Munich, Beck, 2001).

1.e Newspaper publications

1. 'So viel vergessen', *Frankfurter Allgemeine Zeitung*, 25 March 1985.
2. 'Ins Laub', ibid.
3. 'Nichts wie hinaus', *Darmstädter Echo*, 25 March 1985.
4. 'In diesen Mörderzeiten', *Frankfurter Allgemeine Zeitung*, 28 March 1985.
5. 'Vom Wetter', *Neue Zürcher Zeitung*, 13–14 April 1985.
6. 'Im Herbst', ibid.
7. 'Grenzübergang', ibid.
8. 'Letzte Rettung', ibid.
9. 'Parsifal reitet', *Frankfurter Allgemeine Zeitung*, 16 April 1985.
10. 'Viel Glück', *Frankfurter Allgemeine Zeitung*, 24 April 1985.
11. 'Westfälische Himmelfahrt', *Frankfurter Allgemeine Zeitung*, 24 July 1985.
12. 'Was es war', *Frankfurter Allgemeine Zeitung*, 5 July 1985.
13. 'Dementi', *Neue Zürcher Zeitung*, 1 June 1985.
14. 'Über den Sonetteschreiber Brecht', *Frankfurter Allgemeine Zeitung*, 2 September 1985.
15. 'Toter Mann', *Neue Zürcher Zeitung*, 14–15 September 1985.
16. 'Bewerbung', ibid.
17. 'Rückwärts', ibid.
18. 'Türen vernageln', ibid.
19. 'Die Wolken', *Frankfurter Allgemeine Zeitung*, 8 October 1985.
20. 'Zwischenbilanz', *Frankfurter Allgemeine Zeitung*, 25 October 1985.
21. 'Wortlose Zeit', *Frankfurter Allgemeine Zeitung*, 28 October 1985.
22. 'Angebot', *Frankfurter Allgemeine Zeitung*, 6 November 1985.
23. 'Sommernacht am Arno', *Frankfurter Allgemeine Zeitung*, 23 November 1985.
24. 'Wenn ich hinginge', *Frankfurter Allgemeine Zeitung*, 7 January 1986.
25. 'Als es gut war', *Frankfurter Allgemeine Zeitung*, 16 January 1986.
26. 'Mit nichts', *Frankfurter Allgemeine Zeitung*, 7 February 1986.
27. 'Befund', *Frankfurter Allgemeine Zeitung*, 15 April 1986.
28. 'Es wäre schön', *Nürnberger Nachrichten*, 24–5 May 1986.
29. 'Ich bin es, immerhin', *Neue Zürcher Zeitung*, 31 May–1 June 1986.
30. 'Neue Werte', *Frankfurter Allgemeine Zeitung*, 10 September 1986.
31. 'Alptraum', *Frankfurter Allgemeine Zeitung*, 18 September 1986.
32. 'Was weiß ich von Bäumen', *Frankfurter Allgemeine Zeitung*, 31 October 1986.
33. 'Halbes Liebeslied für ganz Berlin', *Neue Zürcher Zeitung*, 28–9 March 1987.
34. 'Wer die Flüsse vertrieb', *Neue Zürcher Zeitung*, 17 June 1987.
35. 'Kreuzberg renoviert', *Neue Zürcher Zeitung*, 23 April 1987.

36. 'Widmung', *Neue Zürcher Zeitung*, 25-6 July 1987.
37. 'Alles vergeht', *Frankfurter Allgemeine Zeitung*, 22 August 1987.
38. 'Benn', *Frankfurter Allgemeine Zeitung*, 27 August 1987.
39. 'Mythos Berlin', *Frankfurter Allgemeine Zeitung*, 20 October 1987.
40. 'Meine Ordnung', *Frankfurter Allgemeine Zeitung*, 30 September 1987.
41. 'Mezzogiorno', *Frankfurter Allgemeine Zeitung*, 23 March 1988.
42. 'Auf die großen Städte', *Frankfurter Allgemeine Zeitung*, 8 January 1988.
43. 'Woyzecks Nachtlied', *Frankfurter Allgemeine Zeitung*, 12 January 1988.
44. 'Schöner Traum', *Frankfurter Allgemeine Zeitung*, 25 June 1988.
45. 'Einsicht', *Frankfurter Allgemeine Zeitung*, 30 August 1988.
46. 'Wiepersdorf, die Arnimschen Gräber', *Frankfurter Allgemeine Zeitung*, 12 September 1988.
47. 'Selbstporträt, korrigiert', *Frankfurter Allgemeine Zeitung*, 19 September 1988.
48. 'Mauergedicht', *Neue Zürcher Zeitung*, 14 February 1990.
49. 'Am Brandenburger Tor', ibid.
50. 'Treffpunkt Oberbaumbrücke', *Neue Zürcher Zeitung*, 7 December 1990.
51. 'Nachtrag', ibid.
52. 'Spaziergang', *Darmstädter Echo*, 9 March 1991.
53. 'Kein Heimgang', *Neue Zürcher Zeitung*, 12-13 January 1992.
54. 'Belcanto', *Neue Zürcher Zeitung*, 20 January 1992.
55. 'Gregor Samsa', *Neue Zürcher Zeitung*, 28 January 1992.
56. 'Im Harz', *Neue Zürcher Zeitung*, 12-13 December 1992.
57. 'Minotaurus', ibid.
58. 'Bits und Bytes', ibid.
59. 'Requiem', *Neue Zürcher Zeitung*, 16 December 1993.
60. 'Heilige Nacht', *Süddeutsche Zeitung Magazin*, Christmas 1993.
61. 'Die Hausgeburt', *Neue Zürcher Zeitung*, 6 February 1996.
62. 'Ankunft in New York', *Neue Zürcher Zeitung*, 28-9 March 1998.
63. 'In Weimar im Winter', *Frankfurter Rundschau*, 2 October 1999.
64. 'Rockefeller Center', *Neue Zürcher Zeitung*, 12 October 1999.
65. 'Lektionen der Leere', *Neue Zürcher Zeitung*, 15 April 2000.
66. 'Rettungsgefühl', *Süddeutsche* Zeitung, 1 July 2000.
67. 'Die Brote der Mutter, *Neue Zürcher Zeitung*, 30 October 2001.
68. 'Schreib-Lähmung', *Tages-Anzeiger*, 3 January 2003.

1.f Interviews

1. '"Der verlorene Sohn". Interview mit Sabine Schmidt', *Rheinische Post*, 25 September 1998.
2. '"Was ich betreibe, ist die Erfindung des Autobiographischen". Gespräch mit Jeanette Stickler', *Frankfurter Rundschau*, 4 March 1998.
3. 'Berlin, lieu étrange et étranger. Propos recueillis et traduits par Nicole Barry', *Page des Libraires. Le magazine des livres*, 60 (November 1999), 52.
4. 'De fortabte. Af Thomas Thurah', *weekendavisen*, 13-19 August 1999.

2. Literary criticism

2.a Books
1. *Fragment ohne Ende. Eine Studie über Wolfgang Koeppen* (Heidelberg, Winter, 1984).
2. *Auslöschungsverfahren. Exemplarische Untersuchungen zur Literatur und Poetik der Moderne* (Munich, Fink, 1995).
3. *Über die Schrift hinaus. Essays zur Literatur* (Frankfurt am Main, Suhrkamp, 2000).

2.b Articles and essays
1. 'Am eigenen Leib. Sinnliche Erfahrung und Ästhetische Wahrnehmung in Peter Weiss' Prosa', in Karl-Heinz Götze and Klaus R. Scherpe (eds), *'Die Ästhetik des Widerstands' lesen* (Berlin, Argument, 1981), 134–45.
2. 'Vom Überdruß leben: Sensibilität und Intellektualität als Ereignis bei Handke, Born und Strauß', [with Klaus R. Scherpe], *Monatshefte*, 73/2 (1982), 187–206.
3. 'Bilder vom letzten Menschen. Anmerkung zum Frühwerk Arno Schmidts', in Jost Hermand, Helmut Peitsch and Klaus R. Scherpe (eds), *Nachkriegsliteratur in Westdeutschland. Bd. 2: Autoren, Sprache, Traditionen* (Berlin, Argument, 1984), 52–64.
4. 'Die Lebendigkeit des Bösen. Zur Gestalt Gottlieb Judejahns in Wolfgang Koeppens Roman *Der Tod in Rom*', *Neue Zürcher Zeitung*, 28–9 September 1985.
5. 'Das Eigene und das Fremde. Türkische Musikkultur in Berlin-Kreuzberg' [with Ahmet Kaya], in Hans Werner Henze (ed.), *Lehrgänge. Erziehung in Musik. Neue Aspekte der musikalischen Ästhetik*, vol. 3 (Frankfurt am Main, Fischer, 1986), 107–32.
6. 'Vom Elend des Schreibens: Franz Kafka und der Hunger der Schrift', *Neue Zürcher Zeitung*, 1–2 November 1986.
7. 'Die Zeit der Poesie' [mit Jens Brockmeier], *Düsseldorfer Debatte*, 12 (1986), 4–14.
8. 'Das Geräusch und das Vergessen. Realitäts- und Geschichtserfahrung in der Nachkriegstrilogie Wolfgang Koeppens', in Eckart Oehlenschläger (ed.), *Wolfgang Koeppen* (Frankfurt am Main, Suhrkamp, 1987), 47–74.
9. 'Über die Schrift hinaus. Franz Kafka, Robert Walser und die Grenzen der Literatur', in Hans-Ulrich Treichel, Jochen Schütze and Dietmar Voss (eds), *Die Fremdheit der Sprache. Studien zur Literatur der Moderne* (Berlin, Argument, 1988), 48–63; reprinted in Klaus Michael Hinz and Thomas Horst (eds), *Robert Walser* (Frankfurt am Main, Suhrkamp, 1991), 292–309.

10. 'Masken der Selbstüberschreitung. Zur erzählenden Prosa und Ästhetik von Yukio Mishima' [with Dietmar Voss], *Merkur*, 3 (1988), 210–24.
11. 'Der Weg zum ungeschriebenen Text. Robert Walsers *Mikrogramme* und die Grenzen der Literatur', *Neue Zürcher Zeitung*, 23–4 April 1988.
12. 'Alfred Andersch und Ernst Jünger. Zur Problemgeschichte einer Anziehungskraft', *Wirkendes Wort*, 39/3 (November–December 1989), 418–27; abridged and reprinted in Justus Fetscher, Eberhard Lämmert and Jürgen Schutte (eds), *Die Gruppe 47 in der Geschichte der Bundesrepublik* (Würzburg, Königshausen & Neumann, 1991), 95–107.
13. 'Schreckliche Suche nach Sinn. Über Yukio Mishima und *Das verratene Meer*', in Hans Werner Henze, *Das verratene Meer. Programmheft* (Berlin, Deutsche Oper, 1990), 25–30.
14. 'Worte, Klänge, Farben. Erkundungen in "Synaesthesia"' [with Jens Brockmeier], in Hans Werner Henze (ed.), *Die Chiffren. Musik und Sprache. Neue Aspekte der musikalischen Ästhetik*, vol. 4 (Frankfurt am Main, Fischer, 1990), 71–120.
15. 'Den Tod täglich ins Herz nehmen. Über Yukio Mishima', *Die Volkszeitung*, 11 May 1990.
16. 'Kein Neuanfang' [on Günter Eich, 'Inventur'], *Frankfurter Allgemeine Zeitung*, 1 December 1990; reprinted in Marcel Reich-Ranicki (ed.), *Frankfurter Anthologie. Gedichte und Interpretationen*, vol. 14 (Frankfurt am Main and Leipzig, Insel, 1991), 209–11; and in Marcel Reich-Ranicki (ed.), *1000 Deutsche Gedichte und ihre Interpretationen*, vol. 8 (Frankfurt am Main and Leipzig, Insel, 1994), 127–9.
17. 'Beißende Zeitkritik, melancholisch grundiert. Zum 85. Geburtstag des Schriftstellers Wolfgang Koeppen', *Der Tagesspiegel*, 23 June 1991.
18. 'Die Geister von Hiddensee. Eine merkwürdige Begegnung mit Asta Nielsen, Joachim Ringelnatz und Gerhart Hauptmann, unweit der Ostsee', *Freitag*, 24 July 1992.
19. 'Das Wagnis der Ankunft' [on August von Platen, 'Sonett XVIII "Mein Auge ließ das hohe Meer zurück"'], *Frankfurter Allgemeine Zeitung*, 19 September 1992; reprinted in Marcel Reich-Ranicki (ed.), *Frankfurter Anthologie. Gedichte und Interpretationen*, vol. 16 (Frankfurt am Main and Leipzig, Insel, 1993), 68–70; also reprinted in Marcel Reich-Ranicki (ed.), *1000 Deutsche Gedichte und ihre Interpretationen*, vol. 3 (Frankfurt am Main and Leipzig, Insel, 1994), 416–8.
20. 'Der Schatten des Verschwindens. Adelbert von Chamisso: *Peter Schlemihls wundersame Geschichte* (1814)', in Winfried Freund (ed.), *Deutsche Novellen* (Munich, Fink, 1993), 37–46.
21. '"Nachgeben an alles, was mich herabziehen will!" Peter Weiss und die Sehnsucht nach der Gestaltlosigkeit', *Neue Zürcher Zeitung*, 5 March 1993.

22. 'Wo der rauhe, böse Lebenskampf regiert. Literaturort Berlin: Robert Walser, sanfter Träumer und Schweizer Bub', *Der Tagesspiegel*, 18 April 1993; reprinted in Günther Rühle (ed.), *LiteraturOrt Berlin* (Berlin, Argon, 1994), 86–90.
23. 'Gesang vom Vergessen' [on Bertolt Brecht, 'Vom ertrunkenen Mädchen'], *Frankfurter Allgemeine Zeitung*, 29 August 1993; reprinted in Marcel Reich-Ranicki (ed.), *Frankfurter Anthologie. Gedichte und Interpretationen*, vol. 17 (Frankfurt am Main and Leipzig, Insel, 1993), 170–1; also reprinted in Marcel Reich-Ranicki (ed.), *1000 Deutsche Gedichte und ihre Interpretationen*, vol. 7 (Frankfurt am Main and Leipzig, Insel, 1994), 324–5.
24. '"Reden die Steine noch?" Zum Bild und zur Wahrnehmung Roms in der deutschen Gegenwartsliteratur', *Neue Rundschau*, 1 (1994), 149–60. [Also *Habilitationsvortrag* held on 16 June 1993 in the Fachbereich Germanistik der Freien Universität Berlin.]
25. 'Ernst Jünger oder Kannibalismus in Steglitz', in Günther Rühle (ed.), *LiteraturOrt Berlin* (Berlin, Argon, 1994), 161–5.
26. 'Mit formvollendeter Beiläufigkeit' [on Rainer Maria Rilke, 'Corrida'], *Frankfurter Allgemeine Zeitung*, 28 May 1994; reprinted in Marcel Reich-Ranicki (ed.), *Frankfurter Anthologie. Gedichte und Interpretationen*, vol. 18 (Frankfurt am Main and Leipzig, Insel, 1995), 115–7; also reprinted in Marcel Reich-Ranicki (ed.), *Rainer Maria Rilke. Und ist ein fest geworden. 33 Gedichte mit Interpretationen* (Frankfurt am Main and Leipzig, Insel, 1996), 45–7.
27. 'Der Gastdozent', *Wochenpost*, 9 June 1994.
28. 'Beherrschung des Elementaren. Zur Aktualität von Ernst Jüngers "Arbeiter"', *Der Tagesspiegel*, 25 July 1994.
29. '"Jeder Schriftsteller ist zweisprachig." Ein Gespräch mit Georges-Arthur Goldschmidt', *Sprache im technischen Zeitalter*, 131 (September 1994), 273–85.
30. 'Harmonie der Kräfte' [on Conrad Ferdinand Meyer, 'Der römische Brunnen'], *Frankfurter Allgemeine Zeitung*, 31 December 1994; reprinted in Marcel Reich-Ranicki (ed.), *Frankfurter Anthologie. Gedichte und Interpretationen*, vol. 18 (Frankfurt am Main and Leipzig, Insel, 1995), 86–8.
31. 'Immerwährender Exodus' [on Paul Celan, 'Auf Reisen'], *Frankfurter Allgemeine Zeitung*, 25 November 1995; reprinted in Marcel Reich-Ranicki (ed.), *Frankfurter Anthologie. Gedichte und Interpretationen*, vol. 19 (Frankfurt am Main and Leipzig, Insel, 1996), 212–14.
32. 'Arbeit am Libretto. Zur Entstehung des Librettos von Hans Werner Henzes Oper "Das verratene Meer"', *Sprache im technischen Zeitalter*, 138 (December 1995), 364–73.
33. 'Johann Christoph Gottsched. "... daß eine gute Schreibart rein, regelmäßig, üblich und deutlich seyn müsse"', in Vera Hauschild (ed.),

Die großen Leipziger. 26 Annäherungen (Frankfurt am Main and Leipzig, Insel, 1996), 86–97.
34. 'Gestalten der Müdigkeit. Zur Ästhetik und Metaphysik eines zweifelhaften Zustands' [with Dietmar Voss], *Annali. Sezione Germanica Universita Orientale Napoli. Nuova serie IV 1994*, 3 (1996), 111–30.
35. 'Wunschtraum eines Ruhelosen' [on Rainer Maria Rilke, 'Römische Fontäne'], *Frankfurter Allgemeine Zeitung*, 24 February 1996; reprinted in Marcel Reich-Ranicki (ed.), *Frankfurter Anthologie. Gedichte und Interpretationen*, vol. 19 (Frankfurt am Main and Leipzig, Insel, 1996), 116–18; also reprinted in Marcel Reich-Ranicki (ed.), *Rainer Maria Rilke. Und ist ein fest geworden. 33 Gedichte mit Interpretationen* (Frankfurt am Main and Leipzig, Insel, 1996), 29–31.
36. 'Der Abgrund ist im Bürger. Eine Erinnerung an Wolfgang Koeppen, der am 15. März in München gestorben ist', *Freitag*, 22 March 1996.
37. 'Dem Kunst-Phallus zugeneigt. Ein Besuch im Berliner Beate-Uhse-Museum', *Neue Zürcher Zeitung*, 22–3 June 1996.
38. 'Die Schule des Librettisten', *Neue Zeitschrift für Musik*, 4 (July–August 1996), 22–4.
39. 'Warum so traurig?' [on Heinrich Heine, 'Die Loreley'], *Frankfurter Allgemeine Zeitung*, 14 December 1996; reprinted in Marcel Reich-Ranicki (ed.), *Frankfurter Anthologie. Gedichte und Interpretationen*, vol. 20 (Frankfurt am Main and Leipzig, Insel, 1997), 65–6; also reprinted in Marcel Reich-Ranicki (ed.), *Heinrich Heine. Ich hab im Traum geweinet. 44 Gedichte mit Interpretationen* (Frankfurt am Main and Leipzig, Insel, 1997), 57–8.
40. 'Adonis in der Eisluft', *Hans Werner Henze. Venus und Adonis. Programmheft der Bayerischen Staatsoper* (Munich, Bayerische Staatsoper, 1997), 23–5.
41. 'Schnee im Pantheon. Michael Krüger: Eine Vorrede', in Walter Hinck (ed.), *Gedichte und Interpretationen*, vol. 7, *Gegenwart II* (Stuttgart, Reclam, 1997), 241–8.
42. '"Wir Rücken an Rücken vereinte". Zeitgeist und Kulturkritik im Werk von Botho Strauß', in Walter Delabar and Erhard Schütz (eds), *Deutschsprachige Literatur der 70er und 80er Jahre. Autoren – Tendenzen – Gattungen* (Darmstadt, Wissenschaftliche Buchgesellschaft, 1997), 286–99.
43. 'Absolut negativ?' [on Heinrich Heine, 'Mein Herz, mein Herz ist traurig'], *Frankfurter Allgemeine Zeitung*, 20 September 1997; reprinted in Marcel Reich-Ranicki (ed.), *Heinrich Heine. Ich hab im Traum geweinet. 44 Gedichte mit Interpretationen* (Frankfurt am Main and Leipzig, Insel, 1997), 64–6; also reprinted in Marcel Reich-Ranicki (ed.), *Frankfurter Anthologie. Gedichte und Interpretationen*, vol. 21 (Frankfurt am Main and Leipzig, Insel, 1998), 69–71.

44. 'Forscher der menschlichen Natur' [obituary for Ernst Jünger], *Der Tagesspiegel*, 18 February 1998; reprinted in Volker Hage, Rainer Moritz and Hubert Winkles (eds), *Deutsche Literatur 1998. Jahresüberblick* (Stuttgart, Reclam, 1999), 57–63.
45. 'Prägende Sätze' [on Martin Walser], *Neue Zürcher Zeitung*, 10–11 October 1998.
46. 'Der schlimme Flötenton. Zum Motiv und zur Bedeutung der Flöte in Kult, Mythologie und Kunst' [with Ulrike Brunotte], in Hans Werner Henze (ed.), *Musik und Mythos. Neue Aspekte der musikalischen Ästhetik*, vol. 5 (Frankfurt am Main, Fischer-Taschenbuch, 1999), 96–115.
47. 'Wolfgang Koeppens italienische Reisen', in Anna Comi and Alexandra Pontzen (eds), *Italien in Deutschland – Deutschland in Italien. Die deutsch-italienischen Wechselbeziehungen in der Belletristik des 20. Jahrhunderts* (Berlin, Erich Schmidt, 1999), 157–68; abridged and reprinted as '"Mit schon gestalteter Empfindung". Wolfgang Koeppens italienische Reisen', *Neue Zürcher Zeitung*, 23–4 January 1999.
48. '"Von mir selber würde ich nie und nimmer reden". Zur Lyrik Hans Magnus Enzensbergers', *Sonderheft Merkur. Lyrik über Lyrik*, 3/4 (March–April 1999), 367–73.
49. '"Als geriete ich selber in Gärung". Über Hoffmansthals *Brief des Lord Chandos*', in Alexander Honold and Manuel Koeppen (eds), *'Die andere Stimme.' Das Fremde in der Kultur der Moderne. Festschrift für Klaus R. Scherpe zum 60. Geburtstag* (Cologne, Weimar and Vienna, Böhlau, 1999), 135–44.
50. 'Die Angst und das Sehen. Über Georges-Arthur Goldschmidts Erzählung "Die Aussetzung"', in Wolfgang Asholt (ed.), *Grenzgänge der Erinnerung. Studien zum Werk von Georges-Arthur Goldschmidt* (Osnabrück, Secolo, 1999), 123–6.
51. 'Vogelfeder ohne Sinn' [on Günter Eich, 'Tage mit Höhern'], *Frankfurter Allgemeine Zeitung*, 3 April 1999; reprinted in Marcel Reich-Ranicki (ed.), *Frankfurter Anthologie. Gedichte und Interpretationen*, vol. 23 (Frankfurt am Main and Leipzig, Insel, 2000), 170–2.
52. 'Kleine Berlinkunde oder Was die Kenner nicht wissen können', *Frankfurter Rundschau*, 15 May 1999.
53. 'Der fehlende Satz. Anmerkung zum Streit um Wolfgang Koeppens Littner-Roman', *Der Tagesspiegel*, 4 September 1999.
54. 'Startigel und Zieligel. Die Methode Enzensbergers: Freundliche Anmerkungen zu seinem 70. Geburtstag am 11. November', *Frankfurter Rundschau*, 6 November 1999.
55. 'Das fremde Tier' [on Georg Trakl, 'In den Nachmittag geflüstert'], *Frankfurter Allgemeine Zeitung*, 11 December 1999; reprinted in Marcel Reich-Ranicki (ed.), *Hundert Gedichte des Jahrhunderts. Mit Interpretationen* (Frankfurt am Main and Leipzig, Insel, 2000), 154–5;

also reprinted in Marcel Reich-Ranicki (ed.), *Frankfurter Anthologie. Gedichte und Interpretationen*, vol. 23 (Frankfurt am Main and Leipzig, Insel, 2000), 110–11.
56. 'Rettungsgefühl', in *50 Jahre Suhrkamp Verlag. Eine Dokumentation zum 1. Juli 2000* (Frankfurt am Main, Suhrkamp, 2000), 52–4.
57. 'Pfeilschnelles Augenblickverschwinden', *die tageszeitung*, 13 May 2000.
58. 'Nur keine Aufregung. Über die Produktivität der Krise von Friedmar Apel', *Frankfurter Allgemeine Zeitung*, 5 August 2000.
59. 'Meine Jahre mit Eberhard Diepgen. Berliner Schriftsteller blicken zurück', *Frankfurter Allgemeine Zeitung*, 16 June 2001.

2.c Radio features

1. 'Näher dem Blut als der Tinte. Möglichkeiten der poetischen Sprache' [with Jens Brockmeier], *Radio Bremen*, 6 December 1981.
2. 'Es gibt schlimmeres als den Weltuntergang. Endzeit und Erlösung im Frühwerk Arno Schmidts', *Radio Bremen*, 12 January 1985.
3. 'Franz Kafka – Die Utopie der Schmerzlosigkeit', *Hessischer Rundfunk*, 1 July 1987.
4. 'Der Autor als Samurai. Yukio Mishima – Ein Schriftsteller der Moderne' [with Dietmar Voss], *Radio Bremen*, 7 February 1988.
5. 'Die Magie der toten Dinge. Ernst Jüngers Naturalienkabinett der Moderne', *Hessischer Rundfunk*, 10 May 1989.
6. 'Abgrund Rom. Bilder der Ewigen Stadt in der Literatur' [mit Ulrike Brunotte], *Hessischer Rundfunk*, 4 October 1994.
7. 'Spiegel – Klangraum – Labyrinth. Annäherungen an die Wasserstadt Venedig' [with Ulrike Brunotte], *Hessischer Rundfunk*, 2 July 1995.
8. 'Zwischen Folter und Erfolg', *Hessischer Rundfunk*, 27 April 1997.
9. 'Die "Loreley" – Geschichte eines Gedichts. Zum 200. Geburtstag von Heinrich Heine' [with Ulrike Brunotte], *Deutschland Radio Berlin*, 12 December 1997.
10. 'Beschwörung, Klage und Verlockung. "Der schlimme Flötenton" in Mythologie, Kunst und Kult' [with Ulrike Brunotte], *Hessischer Rundfunk*, 5 April 1998.
11. '"Ein größenwahnsinnig gewordenes Dorf". Zum Bild New Yorks in der deutschsprachigen Gegenwartsliteratur' [with Ulrike Brunotte], *Hessischer Rundfunk*, 9 May 1999.

2.d Edited volumes

1. *Stadansichten. Gedichte Westberliner Autoren* [with Peter Gerlinghoff and Günther Maschuff] (Berlin, Herrmann, 1977).
2. *Wolfgang Koeppen: Gesammelte Werke in sechs Bänden* [with Marcel Reich-Ranicki and Dagmar Briel] (Frankfurt am Main, Suhrkamp, 1986).
3. *Die Fremdheit der Sprache. Studien zur Literatur der Moderne* [with Jochen Schütze and Dietmar Voss] (Berlin, Argument, 1988).

Bibliography

4. *Wolfgang Koeppen: Einer der schreibt. Gespräche und Interviews* [including introduction] (Frankfurt am Main, Suhrkamp, 1995).
5. *Landschaft mit Leuchtspuren. Neue Texte aus Sachsen* [with Kerstin Keller-Loibl, Helgard Rost and Jörg Schieke] (Leipzig, Reclam, 1999).

2.e Reviews

1. 'Höflichkeit und Herzenstakt. George Steiners Plädoyer für eine neue Moralität der ästhetischen Erfahrung' [on George Steiner, *Von realer Gegenwart. Hat unser Sprechen Inhalt?*], *Die Volkszeitung*, 5 October 1990.
2. 'Chamäleon der Kognition. Wolfgang Isers Perspektiven literarischer Anthropologie' [on Wolfgang Iser, *Das fictive und das Imaginäre. Perspektiven literarischer Anthropologie*], *Freitag*, 27 September 1991.
3. 'Ein Grabstein für die Zukunft' [on Durs Grünbein, *Schädelbasislektion. Gedichte* and Holger Teschke, *Jasmunder Felder – Windschlucht New York. Gedichte*], *Die Welt*, 8 October 1991.
4. 'Wo der Schwingrasen die Füße feucht hält. Sarah Kirschs lyrische Prosa aus Holstein' [on Sarah Kirsch, *Schwingrasen*], *Der Tagesspiegel*, 9 October 1991.
5. 'Last und Lust des Erinnerns. Wolfgang Koeppens Prosafragment *Es war einmal in Masuren*', *Freitag*, 15 November 1991.
6. 'Rekonvaleszent der Klassengesellschaft. Peter Weiss' Tagebücher und eine Werkausgabe', *Der Tagesspiegel*, 1 December 1991.
7. 'Aus einer deutschen Hölle. Spätes Bekenntnis zum eigenen Werk: Wolfgang Koeppen als Autor von *Jakob Littners Aufzeichnungen aus einem Erdloch*', *Freitag*, 6 March 1992.
8. 'Lenin, Leo, Leonardo und ein klassisches österreichisches Trauma. Manfred Mosers intellektueller Heimatroman *Second Land*', *Der Tagesspiegel*, 5 April 1992.
9. 'Ach, Sprache, meine stumme Braut. Lyrik von Werner Lutz und Werner Söllner', *Die Welt*, 18 April 1992.
10. 'Die richtige Menge Chaos. Botho Strauss' Reflexionen und Notizen *Beginnlosigkeit*', *Freitag*, 8 May 1992.
11. 'Rom im Kopf und in den Sinnen. Klaus Modick nimmt Abschied von der Ewigen Stadt', *Der Tagesspiegel*, 17 May 1992.
12. 'Ich finde mich fragend. George Steiner und der zischende Schwenk der Stahlspitze am Federhalter' [on George Steiner, *Unter Druck. Parabeln*], *Der Tagesspiegel*, 23 August 1992.
13. 'Vor Wut schäumt der Poet [on Peter Handke, *Langsam im Schatten. Gesammelte Verzettelungen 1980–91*], *Die Welt*, 29 September 1992.
14. 'Diner mit einem Bären. Neue Gedichte von Sarah Kirsch' [on Sarah Kirsch, *Erlkönigs Tochter*], *Der Tagesspiegel*, 29 September 1992.
15. 'Niedergeschlagene Engel. Aus dem Nachlaß: Heinrich Bölls Roman *Der Engel schwieg*', *Freitag*, 2 October 1992.

16. 'Der Kampf einer Krähe mit dem Rest einer Bratwurst' [on Lukas Hammerstein, *Im freien Fall*], *Der Tagesspiegel*, 6 December 1992.
17. 'Lust der Qual. Goldschmidt erzählt von traumatischen Erfahrungen', [on Georges-Arthur Goldschmidt, *Der unterbrochene Wald*), *Der Tagesspiegel*, 17 January 1993.
18. 'Spiegelscherben eines Melancholikers' [on Heinz Czechowski, *Nachtspur. Gedichte und Prosa 1987–92*], *Die Welt*, 3 April 1993.
19. 'Ein glücklicher Dichter. Vladimir Nabokovs Roman *Die Gabe* erstmals auf deutsch', *Spiegel Spezial*, 5 (1993), 41–3.
20. 'Rom, ein Trödelladen. Der Franzose Julien Gracq, kein Freund der Stadt am Tiber' [on Julien Gracq, *Rom. Um die sieben Hügel*], *Der Tagesspiegel*, 26 September 1993.
21. 'Magie und Katastrophenroulette. Ernst Jüngers drittes Alterstagebuch' [on Ernest Jünger, *Siebzig verweht III*), *Der Tagesspiegel*, 5 December 1993.
22. 'Die weißen Gipfel der Imagination. *Im Dunkeln spielen*. Essays von Toni Morrison', *Freitag*, 18 March 1994.
23. 'Heute wird die Stadt nicht versinken. Wolfgang Koeppen spaziert noch einmal durch Venedig' [on Wolfgang Koeppen, *Ich bin gern in Venedig warum*], *Der Tagesspiegel*, 2–4 April 1994.
24. 'Der fremde furchtbare Blick. Sarah Kirschs neue Posa über das vermeintlich simple Leben' [on Sarah Kirsch, *Das simple Leben*], *Der Tagesspiegel*, 26 June 1994.
25. 'Buchzeit: Antonia Byatt, *Morpho Eugenia*', *Sender Freies Berlin*, 7 July 1994.
26. 'Der Schaumberg Geschichte' [on Kuno Raeber, *Sacco di Roma*], *Zitty*, 17 (1994), 200.
27. 'Brocken aus unserer Urzeit. Auf vertrautem Terrain: Botho Strauß' neue Prosa' [on Botho Strauß, *Wohnen Dämmern Lügen*], *Der Tagesspiegel*, 18 September 1994.
28. 'Liebe und Tortur' [on Gabriel Garcia Marquez, *Von der Liebe und anderen Dämonen*], *Spiegel Spezial*, 2 (October 1994), 55–6.
29. 'Die Hammerschläge des Vaters. David Grossmanns Roman über eine Kindheit in Jerusalem' [on David Grossmann, *Der Kindheitserfinder*], *Freitag*, 25 November 1994.
30. 'Aufbruch ins Fremde. Umberto Eccos neuer Roman *Die Insel des vorigen Tages*', *Freitag*, 24 March 1995.
31. 'Armut und Licht. Albert Camus' unvollendeter Roman *Der erste Mensch*', *Freitag*, 13 October 1995.
32. 'Kind in der Kiste. Lars Gustafssons vorläufige Lebenserinnerungen', *Freitag*, 29 March 1996.
33. 'Weltgemälde aus Wortgeröll. Ingo Schramms Debutroman *Fitachers Blau*', *Neue Zürcher Zeitung*, 18 April 1996.

34. 'Wenn der Hahn dreimal kräht. Fritz Rudolf Fries' Tagebücher *Im Jahr des Hahns*', Neue Zürcher Zeitung, 18–19 May 1996.
35. 'Schuld und Strafe' [on Georges-Arthur Goldschmidt, *Die Aussetzung*], Wochenpost, 22 August 1996.
36. 'Was Schönheit ist, was Schönheit kann. Wolfgang Hildesheimers gesammelte Kunstbetrachtungen' [on Wolfgang Hildesheimer, *Schule des Sehens. Kunstbetrachtungen*], Neue Zürcher Zeitung, 1 October 1996.
37. 'Versöhnliche Erinnerungen. Ludwig Harig über sen Leben in der Nachkriegszeit' [on Ludwig Harig, *Wer mit den Wölfen heult, wird Wolf*], Neue Zürcher Zeitung, 3 October 1996.
38. 'Rauchen in Amerika. Adolf Endler schadet seiner Gesundheit' [on Adolf Endler, *Warnung vor Utah. Momente einer USA-Reise*], Neue Zürcher Zeitung, 3 December 1996.
39. 'Ich denke an Kassel. Gottfried Benns Briefe an Astrid Claes', Neue Zürcher Zeitung, 29 May 1997.
40. 'Andalusische Nachtbar namens Mainz. Vom Verschwinden aus der Zeitungszeit, Peter Handkes neuer Roman *In einer dunklen Nacht ging ich aus meinem stillen Haus*', die tageszeitung, 23 April 1997.
41. 'Das kälteste Land der Welt? Martin Mosebachs italienische Reise' [on Martin Mosebach, *Die schöne Gewohnheit zu leben. Eine italienische Reise*], Neue Zürcher Zeitung, 23–4 August 1997.
42. 'Die Jockeys der Apokalypse. Ludwig Fels jagt den Kinderschänder "Mister Joe"' [on Ludwig Fels, *Mister Joe*], Neue Zürcher Zeitung, 30–1 August 1997.
43. 'Unter den Hunden der Unterhund. Zwei Essyas über Robert Walser' [on William Gass and Jörg Laederach, *Über Robert Walser. Zwei Essays*], Neue Zürcher Zeitung, 25 October 1997.
44. 'Das langsame Schicksal. Siegfried Lenz in einer Werkausgabe' [on Siegfried Lenz, *Werkausgabe in Einzelbänden*, vols 4, 6, 14 and 19], Frankfurter Allgemeine Zeitung, 17 January 1998.
45. '"Keucht woanders." Peter Handkes fortgesetzte Journale' [on Peter Handke, *Am Felsfenster morgens (und andere Ortszeiten 1982–7)*], die tageszeitung, 23 March 1998.
46. 'Nicht Brot noch Wein. Primo Levis Gedichte' [on Primo Levi, *Zu ungewisser Stunde*], Frankfurter Allgemeine Zeitung, 11 April 1998.
47. '"Meine Güte, ich kann ja schreiben!" Neue Bücher über Kreatives Schreiben', Neue Zürcher Zeitung, 4–5 July 1998.
48. 'Der richtige Mann für Gelsenkirchen. Petra Morsbach blickt hinter die Kulissen' [on Petra Morsbach, *Opernroman*], Neue Zürcher Zeitung, 17–18 October 1998.
49. 'Schau abwärts, Engel. Colum McCann untergräbt Amerika' [on Colum McCann, *Der Himmel unter der Stadt*], Frankfurter Allgemeine Zeitung, 31 October 1998.

50. 'Ein frisches Flanellhemd' [on Anne Tyler, *Engel gesucht*], *Frankfurter Allgemeine Zeitung*, 14 November 1998.
51. 'Furor eines Psychopathen' [on T. C. Boyle, *Riven Rock*], *Der Spiegel*, 21 December 1998.
52. 'Doppelt entblößt, doppelt verborgen' [on Georges-Arthur Goldschmidt, *Als Freud das Meer sah. Freud und die deutsche Sprache*], *die tageszeitung*, 25 March 1999.
53. 'Die letzte Reise. Erstmals erschienen: August von Goethes *Auf einer Reise nach Süden*', *Neue Zürcher Zeitung*, 30 April 1999.
54. 'Die Stadt der toten Dichter. Neue Bücher über Weimar' [on Jochen Klaus, *Weimar. Stadt der Dichter, Denker und Mäzene. Von den Anfängen bis zu Goethes Tod*, Peter Merseburger, *Mythos Weimar. Zwischen Geist und Macht* and Thomas Steinfeld, *Weimar. Mit Photographien von Barbara Klemm*], *Neue Zürcher Zeitung*, 22–3 May 1999.
55. 'Die Balance des mittleren Elends. Hermione Lees Biographie über Virginia Woolf' [on Hermione Lee, *Virginia Wolf. Ein Leben*], *Frankfurter Allgemeine Zeitung*, 31 July 1999.
56. '"Diese Buch darf nicht erscheinen!" Briefe von und an Wolfgang Hildesheimer' [on Wolfgang Hildesheimer, *Briefe*], *Neue Zürcher Zeitung*, 12 October 1999.
57. 'Die Aura ausgebleichter Bergspitzen' [on James Salter, *In der Wand*], *Frankfurter Allgemeine Zeitung*, 30 November 1999.
58. 'Venus mit Hirn. Richard Dooling geht ins Labor' [on Richard Dooling, *Watsons Brainstorm*], *Frankfurter Allgemeine Zeitung*, 15 July 2000.
59. 'Auf dem Karussellpferd. Marek Lawrynowicz Polen', *Frankfurter Allgemeine Zeitung*, 21 October 2000.
60. 'Bekennender Hinterwäldler' [on Gerhard Nebel, *Schmerz des Vermissens*], *Neue Zürcher Zeitung*, 10 May 2001.
61. 'Geschichte vom Narr Gottes' [on Stewart O'Nan, *Das Glück der anderen*], *Die Welt*, 29 September 2001.
62. 'Korrekturen des Lebensromans' [on Jörg Döring, *'ich stellte mich unter, ich machte mich klein': Wolfgang Koeppen 1933–48*], *Neue Zürcher Zeitung*, 7 February 2002.
63. 'In der Mitte ein großes Tabu' [on Klaus Briegleb, *Wie antisemitisch war die Gruppe 47*], *Die Welt*, 25 January 2003.
64. 'Was Gottfried will, was Ursel tut. Gottfried Benns Briefe an Ursula Ziebarth', *Neue Zürcher Zeitung*, 17 September 2003.

3. Secondary Literature

1. Anonymous, 'Kaminfeuer der Eitelkeiten', *Focus Magazin*, 28 February 2000.
2. ——, 'Endmoränen. Die besten deutschen Romane des Herbstes' [on *Der irdische Amor*], *Die Welt*, 5 October 2003.

3. Arend, Ingo, 'Ich ist unwahrscheinlich' [on *Der Verlorene*], *Freitag*, 6 March 1998.
4. Auffermann, Verena, 'Neue lieblose Legenden' [on *Heimatkunde*], *Süddeutsche Zeitung*, 27-8 April 1996.
5. ——, 'Das Gespenst der Familie' [on *Der Verlorene*], *Süddeutsche Zeitung*, 7-8 March 1998.
6. ——, 'Wer erzählen kann, hat viel zu tun', *Tages-Anzeiger*, 14 September 2002.
7. Balzer, Jens, 'Flüchtling 2307' [on *Der Verlorene*], *Deutsches Allgemeines Sonntagsblatt*, 27 March 1998.
8. Bartmann, Christoph, 'Großes Ego, kleines Ich', *Die Presse*, 25 March 2000.
9. Bauer, Michael, 'Schrille Stille', *Süddeutsche Zeitung*, 26-7 February 2000.
10. Baureithel, Ulrike, 'Student, dem Vergessen entrissen', *Der Tagesspiegel*, 26 March 2000.
11. Bielefeld, Claus-Ulrich, 'Gegen Schüchternheit hilft nur Literatur', *Tages-Anzeiger*, 23 March 2000.
12. Bormann, Alexander von, 'Nicht nur "künstliche Wunden"' [on *Seit Tagen kein Wunder*], *Neue Zürcher Zeitung*, 26 October 1990.
13. Bucheli, Roman, 'Die offene Wunder Erinnerung' [on *Der irdische Amor*], *Neue Zürcher Zeitung*, 8 October 2002.
14. Demetz, Peter, 'Trümpfe in zögernder Hand' [on *Liebe Not*], *Frankfurter Allgemeine Zeitung*, 5 July 1986.
15. Ebel, Martin, 'Die Suche nach dem Bruder' [on *Der Verlorene*], *Stuttgarter Zeitung*, 5 June 1998.
16. ——, 'In der Komponistenumlaufbahn' [on *Tristanakkord*], *Stuttgarter Zeitung*, 21 March 2000.
17. ——, 'Komisches Scheitern' [on *Der irdische Amor*], *Tages-Anzeiger*, 20 September 2002.
18. Feldmann, Joachim, 'Aus der Kindheit' [on *Der Verlorene*], *Am Erker*, 35 (1998), 115-6.
19. Geitel, Klaus, 'Über Verlockungen, Schriftsteller und die Neue Musik' [on *Tristanakkord*], *Die Welt*, 17 June 2000.
20. Genazino, Wilhelm, 'Komisches Unglück' [on *Der Verlorene*], *Frankfurter Rundschau*, 25 March 1998.
21. Hage, Volker, 'Auf der Suche nach Arnold' [on *Der Verlorene*], *Der Spiegel*, 23 March 1998.
22. Hagestedt, Lutz, 'Wer ist Findelkind 2307?' [on *Der Verlorene*], *Badische Zeitung*, 31 March 1998.
23. Hartung, Harald, 'Die Philosophie zieht in den Garten' [on *Von Leib und Seele*], *Frankfurter Allgemeine Zeitung*, 27 June 1992.
24. Hartwig, Ina, 'Die Fallhöhe der Gemeinheit', *Frankfurter Rundschau*, 4 March 2000.

25. ——, 'Die Messe als moralische Anstalt', *Frankfurter Rundschau*, 24 March 2003.
26. Henning, Peter, 'Irrtümer als Stationen der Wahrheit' [on *Von Leib und Seele*], *Die Weltwoche*, 20 April 1992.
27. Henschel, Gerhard, 'Emsfelde regiert. Der Erzähler Hans-Ulrich Treichel', *Merkur*, 57 (2003), 344–8.
28. Hieber, Jochen, 'Vom Angriff der Wirklichkeit auf das Weltbild der Dichter' [on *Seit Tagen kein Wunder*], *Frankfurter Allgemeine Zeitung*, 24 November 1990.
29. Jacobs, Steffen, 'Stoßgebet. Jacobs' Gedichte (12)', *Die Welt*, 24 November 2002.
30. Jahn, Oliver, 'Aus dem Geist der Langeweile', *Die Welt*, 25 November 2000.
31. Jähner, Harald, 'Aufstrebende Flügelrandschweifungen' [on *Der Verlorene*], *Berliner Zeitung*, 25 April 1998.
32. Jenny-Ebeling, Charitas, 'Flackern im Hirn' [on *Der einzige Gast*], *Neue Zürcher Zeitung*, 8–9 January 1995.
33. Joachimsthaler, Jürgen, '"Der Pole" sieht Polen: Hans-Ulrich Treichel in Lublin', *Germanico-Slavica*, 12 (2000–1), 51–65.
34. Keil, Franz, 'Laß bloß das Fernsehhn nicht ausfallen!', *Die Welt*, 2 June 2001.
35. Kicker, Hergen, 'Tristan profan' [on *Tristanakkord*], *Berliner Morgenpost*, 26 March 2000.
36. Knipphals, Dirk, 'Hohe Schule' [on *Über die Schrift hinaus*], *die tageszeitung*, 24 June 2000.
37. Köhler, Andrea, 'Das kulturelle Gefühl' [on *Tristanakkord*], *Neue Zürcher Zeitung*, 1–2 April 2000.
38. ——, 'Komödie der Triebe. Hans-Ulrich Treichels Roman *Der irdische Amor*', *Neue Zürcher Zeitung*, 8 October 2002.
39. ——, 'Die großen Illusionen und der Katzenjammer', *Frankfurter Allgemeine Zeitung*, 11 October 2003.
40. Kosler, Hans Christian, 'Vom pathologischen Lauf der Welt' [on *Von Leib und Seele*], *Süddeutsche Zeitung*, 5–6 September 1992.
41. ——, 'Kein Verwehn, kein Vergehn' [on *Der einzige Gast*], *Süddeutsche Zeitung*, 31 December 1994–1 January 1995.
42. Kraft, Thomas, 'Heimat im Laufstall', *Freitag*, 26 April 1996.
43. Krätzer, Jürgen, 'Vom Blutsuppenkaspar' [on *Der Verlorene*], *Neue Deutsche Literatur*, 5 (1998), 163–6.
44. Krause, Tilman, 'Erlöst vom Kunstwahn' [on *Tristanakkord*], *Die Welt*, 25 March 2000.
45. ——, 'Immer neue Vergeblichkeiten' [on *Der irdische Amor*], *Die Welt*, 3 August 2003.
46. Kübeler, Gunhild, 'Vermessungswahn' [on *Der Verlorene*], *Die Weltwoche*, 2 April 1998.

47. Kunckel, Susanne, 'Das Leben als unvollendetes Werk', *Die Welt*, 6 April 2003.
48. Kurth, Cornelia, 'Wo die Politik die Literatur umarmt', *die tageszeitung*, 27 January 1993.
49. Löffeler, Sigrid, 'Der untote Bruder' [on *Der Verlorene*], *Die Zeit*, 26 March 1998.
50. Luchsinger, Martin, 'Sarkastiscshe Besichtigungen' [on *Heimatkunde*], *Tages-Anzeiger*, Zürich, 3 May 1996.
51. Lüdke, Martin, 'Die Entdeckung der Anus-Vulva-Achse' [on *Der irdische Amor*], *Die Zeit*, 29 August 2002.
52. Lütkehaus, Ludger, 'Finale Neurosen' [on *Von Leib und Seele*], *Die Zeit*, 8 May 1992.
53. Mack, Gerhard, 'Philosophin lebt aus Plastiktüten' [on *Von Leib und Seele*], *Die Welt*, 25 July 1992.
54. Magenau, Jörg, 'Arbeitsansätze, die an Harndrang scheitern' [on *Heimatkunde*], *Der Tagesspiegel*, 7 April 1996.
55. ——, 'Schamjahre' [on *Der Verlorene*], *die tageszeitung*, 20 March 1998.
56. ——, 'Anekdoten machen das Leben leichter', *Frankfurter Allgemeine Zeitung*, 17 August 2002.
57. Maidt-Zinke, Kristina, 'Wenn du bedürftig bist, sinken deine Chancen' [on *Der irdische Amor*], *Süddeutsche Zeitung*, 6 August 2002.
58. Mazenauer, Beat, 'Gebändigt unerfüllt' [on *Tristanakkord*], *Freitag*, 25 February 2000.
59. Modick, Klaus, 'Die produktive Krise bei Schriftstellern – ein Paradox?', *die tageszeitung*, 25 July 2000.
60. Naumann, Klaus, 'Die neunziger Jahre, ein nervöses Jahrzehnt: deutsche Kriegsbilder am Ende der Nachkriegszeit', in Ursula Heukenkamp (ed.), *Schuld und Sühne? Kriegserlebnis und Kriegsdeutung in deutschen Medien der Nachkriegszeit 1945–61* (Amsterdam, Rodopi, 2001), 801–11.
61. Nickel, Günther, 'Ein irdischer Amor', *Frankfurter Allgemeine Zeitung*, 25 August 2002.
62. Nuber, Achim, 'Hans-Ulrich Treichel: *Der Verlorene*', *Passauer Pegasus* 31–2 (1998), 193–5.
63. Nuber, Albert, 'Kindheit und Jugend im Zeichen von Flucht und Vertreibung. Hans-Ulrich Treichels *Der Verlorene* im Kontext zeitgenössischer Biographieerzählungen', in Sascha Feuert (ed.), *Flucht und Vertreibung in der deutschen Literatur. Beiträge* (Frankfurt am Main, Lang, 2001), 265–80.
64. Overath, Angelika, 'Auch Venedig ist fürchterlich' [on *Heimatkunde*], *Neue Zürcher Zeitung*, 18 June 1996.
65. Plath, Jörg, 'Ein Register der Verheerung' [on *Heimatkunde*], *die tageszeitung*, 23 May 1996.

66. Rathnow, Thomas, 'Das Phantom der Familie' [on *Der Verlorene*], *Der Tagesspiegel*, 14 June 1998.
67. Schäfer, Andreas, 'In der Thomas-Bernhard-Falle' [on *Heimatkunde*], *Berliner Zeitung*, 20 July 1996.
68. Schmidt, Sabine, 'Der verlorene Sohn. Interview' [on *Der Verlorene*], *Rheinische Post*, 25 September 1998.
69. Schneider, Rolf, 'Trend zum Künstlerroman', *Berliner Morgenpost*, 29 December 2000.
70. Schröder, Julia, 'Helden der Beobachtung' [on *Heimatkunde*], *Stuttgarter Zeitung*, 2 August 1996.
71. Schulz, Gerhard, 'Das dauerhafte Grinsen im Opel Admiral' [on *Der Verlorene*], *Frankfurter Allgemeine Zeitung*, 24 March 1998.
72. Schütz, Erhard, 'Gemischte Gefühle, klarer Verstand' [on *Seit Tagen kein Wunder*], *Frankfurter Rundschau*, 23 October 1990.
73. ——, 'Gewissermaßen wie Zecken' [on *Von Leib und Seele*], *Der Tagesspiegel*, 7 June 1992.
74. Schweizer, Michael, 'Staubsauger und Medusa' [on *Von Leib und Seele*], *Freitag*, 5 June 1992.
75. Schütte, Wolfram, 'Schnurriger Humorist' [on *Heimatkunde*], *Frankfurter Rundschau*, 18 May 1996.
76. Steinfeld, Thomas, 'Pappkameraden, westwärts' [on *Tristanakkord*], *Frankfurter Allgemeine Zeitung*, 26 February 2000.
77. Stickler, Jeanette, 'Der Held fährt Trittbrett' [on *Tristanakkord*], *Rheinische Merkur*, 25 February 2000.
78. Taberner, Stuart, 'Hans-Ulrich Treichel's *Der Verlorene* and the problem of German wartime suffering', *Modern Language Review*, 97 (2002), 123–34.
79. Tewinkel, Christiane, 'Libeskranker Bildungsbürger' [on *Der irdische Amor*], *die tageszeitung*, 19 November 2002.
80. Tilman, Krause, 'Erlöst vom Kunstwahn' [on *Tristanakkord*], *Die Welt*, 25 March 2000.
81. Umbach, Klaus, 'Pechvogel trifft Paradiesvogel' [on *Tristanakkord*], *Der Spiegel*, 12 June 2000.
82. Wallmann, Jürgen P., 'Trotz Bier und Brause bei klarem Verstand' [on *Seit Tagen kein Wunder*], *Die Welt*, 4 August 1990.
83. Wapnewski, Peter, 'Spröder Irrwitz' [on *Von Leib und Seele*], *Die Weltwoche*, 1 October 1992.
84. Williams, Rhys W., 'Mein Undewußtes kannte [. . .] den Fall der Mauer und die deutsche Wiedervereinigung nicht': The writer Hans-Ulrich Treichel', *German Life and Letters*, 55 (2002), 208–18.

Index

Adorno, Theodor 14
Alberti, Leon Battista 15
Allen, Woody 87
Andersch, Alfred vii, 40
Die Rote 95, 106
Auslöschungsverfahren. Exemplarische Untersuchungen zur Literatur und Poetik der Moderne 11, 95

Bachmann, Ingeborg 27
Barthes, Roland 72-3
Beethoven, Ludwig van 88
Bellini, Giovanni 99
Benjamin, Walter 14
Benn, Gottfried 14-15, 79
Bernhard, Thomas 79
Beyer, Marcel
Flughunde 22
Bloch, Ernst 14
Bohrer, Karl Heinz 90
Borchers, Elisabeth 15
Boyle, T. C. 79
Brecht, Bertolt 14-15, 25

Callas, Maria 87
Camões, Luis de 46
Camus, Albert 12-13
Cardinale, Claudia 33, 54, 97
Carravaggio x, 33-5, 54, 57, 96-103

Der einzige Gast 10
Der Entwurf des Autors 11, 13, 26-7, 37-42, 57, 61-2, 95, 104
Der irdische Amor x, 11, 33-6, 54-9, 94-110

Der Verlorene x, 11, 21-3, 35, 29, 47-9, 61-78, 80, 82, 86, 95, 97, 103, 105, 108

Eich, Günter 79
Eichendorff, Joseph von 79
Ein Restposten der Zukunft 10, 15
Enzensberger, Hans Magnus 15, 40, 79

Fontane, Theodor 38
Frederick William III 102
Freud, Sigmund 104
Fries, Fritz Rudolf 79

Gespräch unter Bäumen 11
Goethe, Johann Wolfgang von 13, 38, 46, 79, 89
Die Leiden des jungen Werther 89, 94
Grass, Günter
Die Blechtrommel 22
Greiner, Ulrich 91
Grien, Hans Baldung 99
Guistiniani, Vincenzo 102

Handke, Peter 79
Harig, Ludwig 79
Heidegger, Martin 84, 90
Heimatkunde oder Alles ist heiter und edel 11, 20-1, 28-9, 42, 44-7, 68-9, 80
Hemingway, Ernest 38
Hendrix, Jimmy 88
Henze, Hans Werner 24, 32, 81
Heym, Georg 69, 88
Hildesheimer, Wolfgang 79

Index

Hölderlin, Friedrich 52

Jandl, Ernst 15
Johnson, Uwe
 Begleitumstände 27
Jünger, Ernst 18

Kafka, Franz 79, 94
 Die Verwandlung 58, 94
Keller, Gottfried 79
Koeppen, Wolfgang 10, 17–18, 59, 79, 95
 Tauben im Gras 17
 Jugend 17
Kropotkin, Peter 104
 Memoiren eines Revolutionärs 105

Lenz, J. M. R. 38
 Liebe Not 10, 15
Lorca, Federico García 15
Loren, Sophia 33
Lukács, Georg 14

Madonna 87
Malinowski, Bronislaw 104, 105
 Geschlechtstrieb und Verdrängung bei den Primitiven 34
 The Secret Life of Savages in North-Western Melanesia 105
Mann, Thomas 12, 30, 79
Mansfield, Jayne 33
Marcuse, Herbert 12, 104
 Versuch über die Befreiung 105
Marx, Karl 14
McCann, Colum 80
McCartney, Paul 87
Mishima, Yukio 25
Modick, Klaus 36

Nietzsche, Friedrich 90
Novalis 79

Onassis, Aristotle 87

Pasolini, Pier Paolo 54
 Accattone 107
Plutarch 38
Proust, Marcel 83–4

Reich-Ranicki, Marcel 15, 17
Reich, Wilhelm 104
 Die Funktion des Orgasmus 34, 105
 Die sexuelle Revolution 34
Rilke, Rainer Maria 84
Rimbaud, Arthur 25
Rousseau, Jean-Jacques 38
Rubens, Peter Paul 103

Saba, Umberto 15
Salter, James 80
Sartre, Jean-Paul 12, 63–4
Schinkel, Karl Friedrich 102
Schirmang, Jochen 36
Schirrmacher, Frank 90
Schlink, Bernhard
 Der Vorleser 21–2
Schmidt, Arno 79
Schneider, Peter
 Lenz 95, 96
Schramm, Ingo 79
Schwarzenegger, Arnold 87
Sebald, W. G. 79
Seghers, Anna 25
 Seit Tagen kein Wunder 10
Stadler, Arnold 84, 90
Stockhausen, Karlheinz 81
Strauß, Botho 84, 90

Index

Tarantella 10, 15
Tarkovsky, Andrey
  Stalker 107–8
Trakl, Georg 79
Tristanakkord x, 11, 24–6, 30–2, 36, 49–54, 56, 58, 69–70, 79–93, 94, 108
Tyler, Anne 79–80

Über die Schrift hinaus 10, 95
Ungaretti, Giuseppe 15

Van Dyck, Anthony 103
Veronese, Paolo 103
Villa Massimo 10, 19, 38, 40, 41
Von Leib und Seele 10, 18–20, 28, 38, 41, 42–4, 46, 80

Walser, Martin 27, 79, 81–4, 86, 87, 88, 90
  Das Einhorn 83
  Die Verteidigung der Kindheit 84
  Ehen in Philippsburg 81, 82–3
  Ein springender Brunnen 81, 83, 84
  Gallistl'sche Krankheit 82
  Heimatkunde 83
  Heimatlob 83
  Über die Schüchternheit 82
Wagner, Robert 86, 89
Walser, Robert 18, 79
Weiss, Peter 79